NOLS RIVER RESCUE GUIDE

NOLS
RIVER RESCUE GUIDE

Nate Ostis

*Illustrations by Eliza Carver
and Caroline Henley*

STACKPOLE
BOOKS

Published by
STACKPOLE BOOKS
5067 Ritter Road
Mechanicsburg, PA 17055
www.stackpolebooks.com

Printed in the United States of America

10 9 8 7 6 5 4 3 2 1

First edition

Cover design by Samantha Pede
Cover photo by the author
Photos by the author except where noted

FSC
www.fsc.org
MIX
Paper from
responsible sources
FSC® C005010

Library of Congress Cataloging-in-Publication Data

Ostis, Nate.
  NOLS river rescue guide / Nate Ostis ; illustrations by Eliza Carver and Caroline Henley. — First edition.
    pages cm
  Includes index.
  ISBN 978-0-8117-1373-3 (alk. paper)
1. Boats and boating—Safety measures. 2. Rescue work. I. National Outdoor Leadership School (U.S.) II. Title. III. Title: National Outdoor Leadership School river rescue guide. IV. Title: River rescue guide.
  GV777.55.O773 2015
  797.10289—dc23
                              2015007686

Disclaimer

NOLS has been operating on rivers across the world since 1965. The ideas, concepts, and systems illustrated in this book are a sampling of what we have used and know to work well in our contexts. These techniques are applicable in many, but not all, river scenarios. If a technique isn't in this book, that doesn't mean it doesn't work. In fact, there are many great techniques that are *not* in this book. Rescue techniques require a specific set of circumstances and some good luck to be successful. Any activity in a river setting is inherently dangerous, and rescue skills applied inappropriately or by unskilled people may be hazardous to all on the scene. The responsibility is on the reader to develop personal expertise and apply the techniques described appropriately for a given situation.

This book is not an adequate substitute for formal instruction in river rescue, but rather a supplement to it. Any book can help you increase your knowledge, but it takes physical practice in realistic environments to develop expertise. Good coaching from mentors or teachers compounds the learning from this practice. Readers are strongly encouraged to take both a practical hands-on river rescue course and a wilderness first aid course prior to recreating anywhere in or around rivers. Choose your training provider carefully. If you are a recreational river runner, be sure to take a rescue course for river runners, rather than a rescue course designed for firefighters. These techniques are best learned under the guidance of a reputable and qualified instructor. Such courses typically range from one to three days in length and often instill a great deal of confidence and understanding in students. Perhaps the greatest take-home point in all rescue education is the emphasis on preventing these emergencies from happening in the first place. Proactive risk management is key for a fun and enjoyable wilderness experience.

Contents

Acknowledgments

Many thanks to all who love rivers and enjoy having them in their life. It is this culture that we are all collectively a part of that I give my biggest thanks to. I can't imagine my life without rivers or without the people who love to be in them. The pioneers of the river industry provided us all with many valuable lessons and shaped a path that we could all explore. I love the history. I enjoy today. And the best day on the river is clearly the next one.

A big thanks to all the contributing authors of this book who shared their experiences in our River Narratives: Charlie Walbridge, Les Bechdel, John Connelly, Marty McDonnell, Brian Ward, Phil DeRiemer, KT Smith, Jim Coffey, Geoff Kooy, Kent Ford, and Sean and Kristin Bierle.

The team at NOLS was instrumental in the completion of this book. Adam Swisher and Ben Lester shepherded the manuscript through many revisions, Eliza Carver and Caroline Henley made beautiful illustrations, and many, many people gave editorial and design input. Tod Schimelpfenig, Drew Leemon, John Gookin, Brad Christensen, Samantha Pede, Eryn Pierce, Jeff Carty, and Nick Storm deserve particular thanks.

Finally, thanks to the team at Stackpole who stuck with us through this journey. In particular, Judith Schnell and Tim Gahr have been wonderful colleagues.

Introduction

The goal of this book is to generate excitement about identifying your own key areas in need of improvement and taking intentional steps toward greater levels of proficiency. It will also serve as an invaluable tool for many instructors and educators who are elevating risk management practices within their organizations. Before reading this book, consider taking a step back and identifying the learning environment you have created and nurtured. Strive to create a positive learning environment. What makes our training effective is our ability to maintain focus, our capacity for stamina and drive, and our eagerness to have fun throughout. Make sure you and your river team are infected with the contagious theme of enjoyable learning.

Professional rescuers conduct a scene size-up before responding on a river in the Pacific Northwest.

CHAPTER 1

SAFETY VERSUS RISK MANAGEMENT

A River is an Active Avalanche

If you pull your truck over at the top of Teton Pass, Wyoming, in the middle of winter and ask some local skiers if you can join them for the day, they will probably tell you, "No thanks." Most backcountry skiers demand that everyone on the team has both modern avalanche rescue equipment and proper training on its use. They also need to be familiar with each other's skill levels, communication strategies, and experience. They need to be comfortable with how their ski partners manage risks. Yet skiers may not see an avalanche all day long—or all season long, for that matter. Many will go years or even their whole lives without experiencing an avalanche.

Compare this to the average recreationalist found on the river, who often has little or no river rescue training and perhaps only some of the necessary gear to perform adequate rescues. Yet there is a 100-percent chance of an avalanche every day on the river. When we negotiate a river, we must perceive it as navigating through an active avalanche. It's a mountain falling down all around us. Unlike a snow avalanche, a churning river flows all day long.

Here are some points to keep in mind:

1. Rivers deserve respect. Rescuers can be oblivious to the risks and complacent with their skill sets and management strategies.
2. River users can be far less prepared for worst-case scenarios than they think.
3. It is up to all of us to instill and maintain high expectations of the people we operate in rivers with and of ourselves.

■ A RIVER NARRATIVE: THE DAY JOEL DIED

By Jim Coffey

It was an upbeat day in Mexico as our 90-day semester was wrapping up. The students were scheduled to finish their independent travel "River Expedition" section within the next hour or so, and our staff was preparing to pick them up. We looked forward to a final journey with our students on the coast to celebrate their success. Everything had been going exactly to script, just the way we like our programs to run.

Then the phone rang, and our storybook ending came to a grinding halt. It was our students calling in using the satellite phone we issued them: "We have an emergency. Joel's not breathing, and he has no pulse." As a river outfitter and outdoor educator, this is the type of news I dread.

We initiated our crisis management procedures and drove to the evacuation point 8 kilometers down a dirt road through sugar cane and mango plantations. The road was rough and thick with brush. We honked the horn relentlessly to declare our presence and attract the group to our location. My mind was swimming with thoughts. How do we manage the well-being of our students? Joel's family? The staff? And at the same time, what happened?

As a final "self-guided" exam—the culmination of three solid months of whitewater guide training—our students were running the final 5 kilometers of a 67 kilometer Class III-IV river. They had four rafts and four kayaks. Prior to the semester most of the students had not had any first aid, CPR, swiftwater rescue, or boating experience.

Nearing the end of the journey, the group entered a Class II section. Joel capsized his kayak and made no attempt to roll up. Another kayaker pulled him out of his boat and dragged him to shore. With signs of life absent, the kayaker started CPR. The rafts arrived on scene, one of them equipped with an AED. We had carried that AED with us around the world, but until now, had never used it. The group had done numerous scenarios and simulations throughout the semester that included unresponsive patients and the use of defibrillation. After being advised to deliver two shocks, Joel's pulse returned. Students started assisting him with rescue breathing while the others organized the evacuation.

We rendezvoused with the students at the trailhead. Joel still required rescue breathing. We added supplemental oxygen, loaded him into the van, and took off for the nearest hospital in Xalapa, almost an hour away. Upon arrival in the ER, Joel was placed in critical care and within 48 hours was airlifted to his home country of Canada, where he has made a complete recovery.

We had plenty of good luck contributing to this fortunate ending, but preparation, practice, and proper equipment all contributed to our success. Working on a dead fellow student was a surreal experience for this group, but they were able to keep clear heads and get Joel the best possible care.

Jim Coffey is the Director of Esprit Whitewater and the WILD Semester (Whitewater Intensive Leadership Development School). ■

The Difference Between Safety and Risk Management

When people return from the river and they report, "Everything went well. We ran a safe trip," what they often really mean is that their experience was uneventful. Certainly talent, skills, and intentional strategy played a role in their success. But we should not be fooled that we somehow provided for complete safety of all those involved in traveling through an active avalanche.

We should not overlook the luck that accompanies us on the river. The inherent risk involved with moving water will always be there no matter what we do. In truth, we cannot provide safety for anyone on a river. Rivers are continuous avalanches, flowing over jagged rocks, and carrying with them rocks, trees, rebar, fence posts, barbed wire, tires, toilets, fishing lines and hooks, bridge parts, and vehicles. Safety is an illusion. There is always risk involved, and our risk management can always improve.

The language we choose impacts and shapes our thinking. Deliberately choose between "safety" and "risk management" in your speech. Empower and enable all members of your group to embrace the concept of teamwork in a river environment by focusing on risk management strategies collectively, versus simply telling everyone they need to be "safe" on the river.

Rivers are dynamic environments. Take advantage of opportunities to look ahead and plan your next moves.

Scouting rapids and conducting adequate scene size-ups are critical skills for rescuers to have.
SACHA JACKSON

Much of the enchantment of adventure is derived from living and traveling in wild places. Wild places are not safe. The word "safety" implies freedom from risk, and in the wonderful, magical chaos of the wilderness, we know safety to be unattainable. We cannot provide safety on a river. What we do is manage risk. More specifically, we manage people.

The Complacency Cycle

River users must guard against complacency. Complacency is an effective buzzword in our discussions, briefings, and goal-setting sessions. We cannot expect to eliminate or avoid complacency completely; perhaps a healthier approach is to realize that complacency is simply a companion that travels with us throughout life. Hopefully, it is not riding alongside you all day, but it will appear regularly for all of us. The real trick is to recognize when it has arrived and adapt effectively before complacency results in an incident or tragedy.

We see complacency everywhere, every day. Expert carpenters lose fingers to table saws every year. Novice woodworkers who are trained well are usually excellent at maintaining safety parameters around the table saw because they are terrified of it. But the more cuts we make, the more comfortable we get, and the more likely we are to drop our defenses. We become more relaxed in that dangerous environment, and that's when we lose fingers. In a river context, that's when people can get seriously injured or killed. It happens in the blink of an eye—just like a table saw accident.

The longer you are in a trade, the more wisdom you've gained, and the more you are perceived as an expert. But you're also arguably more susceptible to complacency than any novice on your team, and, therefore, potentially just as much of a liability as that novice. Being prepared for river rescue requires intentional planning and constant training to elevate and maintain your skill base. It takes a group mentality that we need to mitigate risks and keep watch on our own complacency.

Other Factors Contributing to River Incidents

There are many factors that can lead us to not paying careful attention to the situation at hand. In addition to complacency, common elements found in backcountry incidents include fatigue, overconfidence, and distraction. For some, the 4:00 p.m. witching hour is the most dangerous time of day. Many folks are tired and a little grouchy. They have been under the sun all day and are a bit dehydrated. Others get hungry and lose focus just before lunch. Or just after lunch due to food-induced brain shutdowns.

Some people report that complacency occurs for them at all different times of the day, with no real pattern to speak of. Too many compromises are made and shortcuts taken on basic risk management strategies. Glaringly obvious oversights are occurring, yet no one seems to notice. Personal flotation devices are no longer fastened properly, or helmets are forgotten. Communication amongst team members effectively ceases to exist, and lack of focus results in poor performance. These are often the moments when incidents occur and people get hurt. Situational awareness is critical for recognizing when these risk factors are present.

Are you really ready? This is one of those questions with no real answer. It's a question that deserves attention and transparency within your team. Ask the questions out loud, "Are we ready? Why? What steps have we taken lately to test or account for our declared level of skill?" Train for the worst and hope for the best. Sharpen the lens that you view the environment through. Assess your present ability levels accurately and honestly.

The Evolution of a Rescuer

It can be helpful to understand and identify your own evolution as a developing rescuer. What progression have you taken to reach your present level? Has this been a simple linear process, or have you traveled through

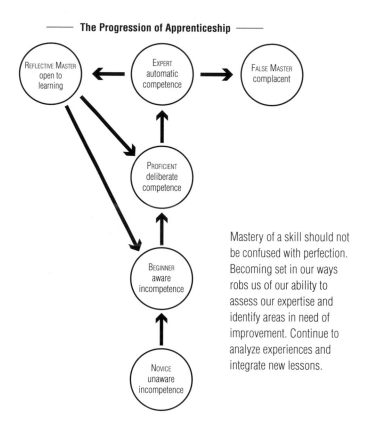

The Progression of Apprenticeship

Mastery of a skill should not be confused with perfection. Becoming set in our ways robs us of our ability to assess our expertise and identify areas in need of improvement. Continue to analyze experiences and integrate new lessons.

patterns and cycles typical of others doing the same thing that you are doing? How do you prevent patterns from repeating themselves?

The progression of apprenticeship from novice to master describes the stages a learner travels through when tackling a new skill set. We begin as a novice, unaware of our incompetence. We don't know what we don't know. As training progresses, we become beginners—aware of our incompetence. We understand what we don't know and what needs to be practiced. After hours of practice and coaching, we become deliberately competent at our new skill. We can demonstrate upon demand, and know that we have the skills. We are proficient. Finally, upon reaching expert status—commonly defined as 10,000 hours of practice in a given skill—autonomy is achieved. We perform automatically, without having to think through each step. However, the automatic responses of the expert have both value and danger. They allow for high levels of performance, but at the same time, they mute the thoughtfulness that helps us calibrate our competence.

Managing pinned boats can be challenging. After you've dealt with the situation, take time to reflect on the causes. Learn from the experience. NATHAN STEWART

Learning does not end when we become experts. False mastery of a skill means the unwillingness to change our approach based on new experiences. In the context of learning, an unwillingness to constantly examine our competence allows that competence to deteriorate over time. Becoming set in our ways inhibits our ability to respond to change. True mastery of a skill involves constantly reflecting on experiences and integrating the lessons into our approach. True mastery means constantly reentering the progression of apprenticeship; in some ways, true masters see themselves as perpetual novices.

■ A RIVER NARRATIVE:
THE RIVER KNOWS NO EXPERTS

By Brian Ward

The North Fork Payette is one of the hardest Class V whitewater runs in North America. When we put into it in June 2011, my friend and I each had multiple years of experience, training, and skills to be kayaking this section of whitewater.

Seven miles into the adventure, my friend suddenly became caught in an enormous hydraulic. He made every attempt to free himself from the churning whitewater, but after many failed attempts was forced to pull his spray skirt and swim. Sitting in the eddy below, I watched his boat race downstream. Soon, he followed. He was too weak to self-rescue, and I would have only one attempt to help him. I paddled close to his course, and as he passed, he reached for the grab handle on my boat. But he was too weak to grab ahold. What followed next was a battle for survival.

He floated head-up into the next rapid, but was running out of energy to swim. Staying on line, I continued to follow, hoping that somehow the river gods would have mercy and release him into the eddy below. This was not the case, and he floated swiftly straight into yet another Class V section.

I paddled out of the eddy and spotted him downstream floating head-down. At the bottom of the rapid, a large wave engulfed him, and he disappeared from sight. I eddied out waiting for him to resurface. His boat and paddle floated by, but no sign of my friend.

I blew my whistle, yelled his name, and scanned the river for an intense five minutes, then quickly ascended the river bank to the road above. Within seconds of reaching the road, I found help from a friend and local paddler who called search and rescue. Kayakers, police, and search and rescue technicians searched the river and its banks for hours.

We started with the last spot where he'd been seen and quickly headed downstream looking at every rock, strainer, and eddy we passed. We found his gear fairly quickly. First his boat, an hour later his paddle, and two hours later his PFD. It would be two weeks before his body was found.

We had scouted the river, had all the proper gear, and were experts in the sport. But the river didn't know we were experts, how much training we had, or how much we loved kayaking. It did demonstrate its ultimate power.

Brian Ward is an accomplished whitewater kayaker and explorer. He is a swiftwater rescue technician and a wilderness first responder. He resides in McCall, Idaho, and owns BReal Media. ■

CHAPTER 2

CREATING A CULTURE OF RISK MANAGEMENT IN THE RIVER ENVIRONMENT

Risk Management is a Culture, Not a Checklist

Individuals and organizations should understand that risk management is a culture, not a checklist. This culture isn't created by accident or happenstance; it's an intentional process that is nurtured and maintained only through constant attention.

Too often, boaters are focused on when their rescue or first aid certifications expire—rather than asking themselves how well they could perform under pressure *right now*. Federal land management agencies can require that you carry a throw bag, a knife, a whistle, a first aid kit, and a pin kit on your river trip. And so you meet these criteria and launch into the river. But is your knife sharp? Does everyone on the trip understand the different whistle signals and how to acknowledge them and relay them to other boats? When was the last time you threw a rope overhand? Underhand? Used butterfly coils? Do you know what is in your first aid kit right now? When was the last time you set up a 3:1 Z-drag? A simple 5:1 system? A compound 9:1 system? When was the last time you practiced a first aid assessment? Or built a splint? How much conversation occurred prior to getting into the river? How many people spoke up or contributed to that conversation?

We've chosen to train as rescuers and first responders. With this comes the challenge to do good work and maintain our skills. Sticking to the basics and our practiced systems, keeping skills sharp with refresher training, maintaining situational awareness, and keeping our cool will help us respond with confidence in an emergency. But just as much attention should be spent on identifying with the culture within our team and how effectively that culture contributes to successful risk management and prevention.

Risk management is a culture, not a checklist. It's an ongoing journey, not a destination.

Outfitting the whole team with proper safety gear can help create a strong culture of risk management.

Prevention is a Critical Leadership Skill

Strive to be more intentional with your planning, and emphasize prevention in group discussions and modeled behavior. Everyone should be anticipating contingencies and making calculated adjustments to the plan. Having all rescue and first aid credentials up to date is important, but practicing the skills regularly is what will make the difference in a true emergency. Successful pre-planning means, "Train for the worst, hope for the best."

Taking a three-day river rescue course or a ten-day wilderness first responder course gives a true appreciation for just how difficult rescues can be, and how much circumstance needs to be on your side for success. These courses teach and emphasize prevention and group awareness. The

"There are old boaters and there are bold boaters.
But there are no old, bold boaters."
—Slightly modified saying of
NOLS founder Paul Petzoldt

more team members with this level of insight, the more each team member can lead herself—making informed decisions that help the group as a whole prevent having "one of those bad days."

Never Underestimate Your Own Ability to be Completely Wrong

This statement perhaps belongs in the disclaimer for this book. Sometimes, we try our best and amazing things happen. Other times, we try our best and everything seems to go wrong. Positive affirmations have tremendous value in building confidence. So does keeping your feet on the ground with a high level of humility. There is only so much room for pride when it comes to rescue. Be the first one to say, "I was wrong." When we do something enough, we tend to believe that we've got it all figured out. We are lucky when we realize that it's only a matter of time before we're wrong about something again. Anticipate the ups and downs. Forgive yourself. Empathize with others. Be sure to enjoy the process. This is a great ride we're on, and the sooner you forget that, the sooner you become unable to impassion others.

Deliberate Team Building

Share knowledge and experience:
- Don't act in isolation.
- Use your team's skills, experience, and knowledge.
- Teaching strengthens the team.
- Ongoing training and practice are critical.

Sometimes the best person to teach a skill is the one who needs the most work on it. So you want to facilitate a practice session on throw bag use? Great! Take a novice team member and coach him or her to deliver a progression to your group. As a group, make a conscious, intentional decision that your number-one goal is to create a team that manages risk effectively using a healthy culture of awareness. And if that is in fact genuinely your goal, then back it up by supporting others in unfamiliar situations.

> "Tell me, and I'll forget.
> Show me, and I may remember.
> Involve me, and I'll understand."
> —Chinese proverb

Conflict Management

Managing conflict starts with the knowledge that conflict *will* occur. This is especially true in rescue situations. If we know conflict is on its way, we can simply say hello to it and address its needs. Much conflict stems from people not understanding their role or what is expected of them. Take a deep breath, and step back. Don't take it personally. Spread calm. Be direct and courteous at the same time. Then re-establish roles, tasks, and expectations.

> "People will forget what you said.
> People will forget what you did.
> But people will never forget how you made them feel."
> —Maya Angelou

Rescue Behavior

The concept of rescue behavior is ideally a discussion point for you and your team prior to engaging in any experience on the river. Real-life rescue situations are overwhelmed with emotion, stress, and fear. It is important that everyone agrees to attempt their best rescue behavior should the need arise. Have your team contribute to creating the list of traits that they feel is typical of exemplary rescue behavior. This stuff isn't rocket science. We all know the things that are likely to be on this list:

- Serve the mission.
- Treat one another with dignity and respect.
- Support leadership. Demonstrate quality followership.
- Trust the team. Trust yourself.
- Embrace fear. Spread calm.
- Go slow to go fast.
- No freelancing.
- Mistakes will occur. Accept them when they happen. Judge them later.
- Tolerate adversity and uncertainty.
- Be honest and accountable.
- Apologize when your attitude has a negative impact on the mission.
- There are no small roles. All tasks assigned are important.
- Know your job and do it.

Boaters versus Floaters

Have I done anything lately to elevate or challenge my skill set? This question is perhaps the simplest differentiation between *boaters* and *floaters*. These are terms that many use synonymously, but which deserve different definitions in order to change perspective on approaches to river running.

Floaters enter the river and simply allow gravity to deliver them to the take-out—they float. They do not conduct adequate safety briefings, nor do they have all the appropriate gear or know how to use it effectively. They may even indulge in alcoholic beverages while negotiating whitewater. They are sometimes overconfident and unwilling to be coached. They simply float through rapids rather than push themselves to make challenging moves and increase their skills. They hardly ever throw their throw bag or practice a swim through a challenging rapid. They may own rescue kits but do not understand how to set up an adequate mechanical advantage system that minimizes risk to all on the scene. They may even have taken a river rescue or wilderness first aid course in the past, but it has been years since they have practiced any of it.

Many believe the expiration date on their training card means they are "current." But certification cards and expiration dates associated with training have little value if all the skills are forgotten or poorly demonstrated; to be current means to be practiced and able to demonstrate the skills effectively when it really matters. Floaters often equate getting to the take-out without injury as an affirmation that they did everything right. They over-internalize credit for success and over-externalize blame for mishaps. They are a liability to themselves, to others, and to the river environment. They are often nice people with big hearts and loving friends and family. Some of your favorite river companions could be floaters.

Boaters are humble and never satisfied with their present skill set or that of those around them. They don't just float downstream—they charge and get after it. They appreciate and acknowledge that both well-practiced skill and good fortune contribute to navigating rivers successfully. They launch on the river with all the appropriate equipment, rescue gear, and first aid supplies. They've been trained effectively and practice their skills regularly, at least every season, if not every trip. Boaters have wilderness first aid training (see first aid section examples). They coach others effectively while soliciting and accepting feedback with appreciation, even from novice team members.

Boaters make challenging moves even when going through relatively easy rapids just to test their skills. They swim whitewater intentionally on a regular basis because they know that is one of the best ways to prepare for incidents in the river. They practice throwing their ropes every day on

Make training fun, and strive to practice some element of rescue each time you go to the river.

the river, even if they are not thrown to anyone in particular. They practice tying knots and building anchors. They can describe and demonstrate the difference between a load-sharing and a load-distributing anchor system. They can build a simple 3:1 mechanical advantage with a redirect in less than five minutes, and can convert that into a compound 9:1 in only three more minutes. They understand what types and placements of carabiners can be dangerous.

Boaters get complacent just like anybody else, and they make mistakes just like anybody else. But with experience, they recognize the symptoms of complacency within themselves and react accordingly. Boaters don't ignore the signs and symptoms of complacency or of a river culture that is not conducive to effective risk management. Boaters can successfully coach and convert floaters to adopt new ways of thinking and can provide a new lens through which to view the river.

Beware of YAMs and OCPs

YAMs—Young Aggressive Males. Rescue and first aid curriculums focus on prevention. Be aware of the aggressive males in your group and prevent them from adding to the statistics. Of course women can and do make aggressive decisions leading to disaster just like men do. This acronym—YAM—is simply an attempt to bring humor to this element of the risk management conversation. Be sure to make training fun and enjoyable. Be just as willing to make fun of yourself as of others.

OCPs—Old Crusty People.
Another silly attempt at humor, this acronym targets those individuals who are susceptible to burnout. OCPs don't necessarily need to be old in age; rather they are stale in perspective. An OCP could be a twenty-eight-year-old river guide that has been guiding for ten con-secutive seasons with the same crew on the same river. An OCP may be overheard saying, "This is the way we've always done it. We don't need any young folks coming in here and changing things up on us." Meanwhile curriculum, tech-niques, and technology have contin-ued to evolve without the OCPs. They're like an expired pack of bat-teries: They once had the energy and passion to drive life forward. Then they shifted into cruise con-trol somewhere along the line, and now it appears they're parked with the emergency brake on.

Wearing appropriate personal protective equipment is just as important as having fun on the river.

To avoid becoming an OCP, demonstrate a commitment to keep things fresh, to remain humble, and to enjoy flexibility by welcoming new ideas and perspectives. Don't feel threatened by young folks. Be secure and encourage their inquisitive nature. We all know folks on our teams who are not bringing their "A" game to the table. If you're not telling them, then you are enabling them and contributing to the problem. If you can't defuse the dynamics on a team in normal conditions, how can you do it in a crisis?

LOOK FOR RED FLAGS

People remember what they want to remember. When listening to a YAM's storytelling, you can often boil down a thirty-minute tale to "It was huge, and I was awesome!" When an OCP gives a response it can often be sum-marized as "Change threatens me." A healthy team will have some aggres-siveness on it, and some conservative, seasoned wisdom, too. But problems occur when the scales get tipped too far in one direction or the

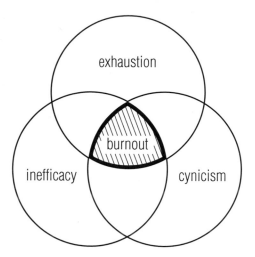

Fatigue, lack of recent success, and an inclination to believe that people are motivated purely by self-interest can all lead to burnout and ultimately poison the culture of risk management on your team. Look for red flags and address them in a timely, growth-oriented manner.

other. It's about finding the right balance and knowing when and how to speak to cultural issues effectively.

Many people arrive at the river for the first time with apprehensions and misconceptions about what is and isn't safe in a river environment. Leaders can insulate their teams from unnecessary stress and misdirected fear by teaching skills in a logical, reassuring progression. Maintaining a high regard for safety precautions, decision-making, and judgment establishes a solid foundation for a comfortable and positive learning environment. Below are some tools for consideration when attempting to put team members at ease.

Five Manageable Risks in the River

These five preventable leading causes of drowning give rivers a risky reputation, but remember that they are preventable. This list was generated by the non-profit organization American Whitewater (americanwhitewater.org). Drowning consistently ranks in the top ten causes of accidental death in the United States every year. In many cases one or more of these following five elements are present:

1. Alcohol: 50 percent of drowning victims have alcohol in their systems. Avoid alcohol when recreating in a river. The chance of injury or death increases significantly once alcohol comes into the equation. Patients with alcohol in their systems often vomit when swimming through a wave train or rapid. People who have aspirated vomit have introduced stomach acids into their lung tissue, which can cause further complications and damage.

2. PFD: Many drowning victims are not wearing a well-fitted personal flotation device (PFD). These are also often referred to as life jackets, but it's important to appreciate that this tool by itself will not save your life. Reasonable judgment and decision-making must also be present. Just because you have a life jacket on doesn't mean you can get away with drinking alcohol while boating or diving into rivers headfirst.

3. Education: In most whitewater incidents, the victims have no prior river education. Give rivers the respect they deserve by seeking out reputable instruction as well as the vast library of effective websites, videos, books, and articles on boating and swiftwater rescue skills.

4. Floods: Flooded rivers claim many lives, both boaters and non-boaters. Floods are the largest contributor to storm-related river deaths in the United States. Helical flows (see Chapter 6) can keep swimmers from getting to shore and result in many flush drownings. Many boaters make the mistake of assuming big water means rapids have washed out or filled in, and are therefore easier. See the "Big Water" section on page 106 for more insight on the dangers of flooded river travel.

NOLS instructors conduct river rescue training in Colorado with an air temperature of 18 degrees, 40-mile-per-hour winds, and 36-degree water temperature.

5. Hypothermia: A common mistake is to dress for air temperature versus water temperature. Have the appropriate gear. We are all in between swims on a river. We've swum before, and we are going to swim again. Some are planned, others happen unexpectedly. Be prepared for the worst-case scenario while remaining optimistic about your success on the river.

Embrace Your Fear

Fear is a naturally occurring, deeply ingrained defensive mechanism designed to protect us from danger. There was a popular bumper sticker/T-shirt that came out in the early 1990s using the simple phrase "No Fear." This is one of many examples of how society has misguided our perceptions of fear and adventure sports. Many people have the impression that fear and being scared are embarrassing emotions for an individual to have. Consider adopting a different culture: "Embrace your fear." Embracing fear means admitting to yourself and possibly others when you are scared. But you might describe your feelings as extra energy rather than overwhelming nervousness. Embrace your fear. And be sure to embrace other people's fear.

Among the physiological effects of stress are the "fight, flight, or freeze" response. In moments of stress, it can be challenging to think

Fear is good. Embrace your fear. Channel the energy in a positive direction.

Rescue scenes can be immersed in visual distractions. Focus on the task at hand while visualizing the positive outcome.

clearly and rationally. How we remain focused during this surge of energy is unique to each of us. Differentiating between good fear and bad fear is an effective tool developed by William Nealy in his book, *Kayak*.

Bad fear occurs when confusion and a lack of specific understanding allow the mind to manufacture anxiety and panic. A rescuer with bad fear may exhibit a stiff upper body, flailing swim strokes, aggressive communication, and an overall frantic demeanor. Training and skills are forgotten as terror overwhelms the mind. Sometimes bad fear will result in a rescuer "freezing up" and taking no action at all.

Good fear, on the other hand, will get a rescuer keyed up, but will not overcome her ability to rationalize and perform. She may have butterflies in the belly and electricity running through her veins, but she can channel her energies in a way that positively impacts the outcome of the situation. A great routine question on any river is, "Are you scared or nervous?" If the answer is yes, hopefully, your follow-up response is, "Good. Me too." Avoid traveling with anyone who says they are *never* scared or who exhibits a reckless approach to the river environment.

A rescue is by its very nature an adverse situation. This is where our true colors often shine through. Stress isn't necessarily a bad thing, so long as it does not negatively impact the rescue team environment. Be ready for many of your ideas to produce little or no results. Stay positive and keep trying. Tolerance for adversity and uncertainty is a critical leadership skill.

It's not necessary to be certain of the solution; there is much gray area in rescue, and a definitive solution can be elusive. It's common to have a list of possibilities and attempt all of them. It's actually a good thing if you or your team feel a twinge of inadequacy about river rescue. That feeling should be there since, in reality, none of us are fully prepared for everything that could happen in the dynamic river environment. If we convince ourselves that we do have all the answers, then we've become a liability, not an asset.

Don't worry about the perfect path; seek choices that work. Try to slow things down. Trust your training, focus on the basics, and maintain big-picture situational awareness. Demonstrate a tolerance for adversity and uncertainty. Remember all of this by simply telling yourself:

Slow is smooth, and smooth is fast.

Or even more simply put:

Go slow to go fast.

Positive Targeting

Beginners tend to look at hazards they are trying to avoid and ultimately end up swimming or paddling right where they don't want to be. Instead, keep your eyes on the prize. Spot your target, and work aggressively towards it. Coach your team to practice positive targeting before entering rapids or anytime they are about to exit their comfort zone. Have them

Make challenging moves in reasonable terrain to increase your skills and develop confidence.

visualize and focus on past successes rather than dwelling on the worst-case scenario. Recite recent teaching cues, positive reinforcements, and affirmations. Generate contingency planning, and be ready and unsurprised to implement Plan B, Plan C, and so on.

Increase confidence by challenging yourself to make hard moves in easy rapids. This simple concept is one of the best ways to become a more proficient rescuer and whitewater paddler. Avoid just floating through a set of waves or lazily swimming a rapid and letting gravity do most of the work. Play "follow the leader" as you swim from one rock to another. Make Class III moves in Class II rapids. Then when you are in a Class III, it isn't as overwhelming because you've already learned what you are capable of in more forgiving terrain. Make the training both fun and challenging. Knowing your ability and matching it to appropriate rivers, rapids, and features ensures calculated, confident rescue responses.

Incident Reviews

Reviewing and reflecting on river incidents can take many forms. Sometimes it can take a very informal form, such as a story floating through the rumor mill, with individuals passing along their versions and their reactions. It could be watching an evening news story on television about some people who got into trouble on the river, or reading an article in a magazine or online. Or it might mean reviewing documents that were written up by an organization in the aftermath of an event on the river.

Many organizations require an incident report anytime an injury or death occurs. Why aren't these forms called "accident reports?" Quiz your teammates at your next risk management meeting, and see how many of them can articulate the difference between an accident and an incident. Take home points of the discussion ideally bring it back to the key concept of intentional nomenclature and its effect on our thinking and decision-making.

ACCIDENT VERSUS INCIDENT

When something goes wrong on the river, it's often called an "accident." In reality, many of the "accidents" are foreseeable. For example, most river injuries occur on slippery and unstable shores. Falls on riverbanks can sprain ankles, break bones, and cause head injuries. So to fall on a riverbank without a helmet on and call the resulting head injury an accident would be a mistake. When these types of things happen again and again, we need to ask ourselves if they really are unforeseeable. Determine if they stem from risks that can be mitigated and effectively managed.

Refine your skill sets in a simulated scenario to increase your awareness and confidence.

Incident is perhaps a more useful term to refer to mishaps on the river. Drew Leemon, NOLS risk management director, states that referring to outdoor mishaps as incidents, "allows us to refer to events in a more factual way. Incident is a nonjudgmental term to refer to events that may be accidental, intentional, a force of nature, errors in judgment or procedures, or an outcome of the inherent risks of participating in adventure activities."

REVIEW PROCESS CONSIDERATIONS
Anyone who intends to recreate in rivers or respond in swiftwater rescues should make a practice of researching recent incidents on the river. Anecdotal learning can be a powerful tool to test your readiness. If you don't know what else has happened out there in the world of rivers, how do you know you won't repeat the mistakes of others? How will you know if you're ready to handle the mishaps that others have already learned from? Unfortunately, it is not uncommon to hear about one particular hazard, such as a strainer, on one specific section of river killing or injuring multiple people on different days within the same season. Had these individuals done their research, they might have learned of this hazard and taken appropriate steps to avoid an incident.

Consider setting up a reminder on your electronic calendar to check for river incidents at least twice a month during your river season. Get the rest of your team on a similar, but offset, schedule, and the chances of you all staying up-to-date on new events will increase dramatically.

Be proactive and train regularly. Share ideas and get excited, about elevating your skills.

Numerous resources exist on the Internet that can be of service for sharing lessons learned. American Whitewater has a boating incident database on its website, which shares a synopsis of individual incidents and the outcomes for the patients involved. Professional rescuers can get incident information through sites like firefighterclosecalls.com. YouTube and Vimeo can also be great resources for finding videos of river rescue. Videos with learning potential should be shared among your community. Ask your team, "How would we do if this was us?" and "Is there something we can do at our next swiftwater training to better prepare ourselves for a situation similar to this one?"

When it comes to reviewing river incidents, there are some key considerations to keep in mind. Appreciate that hindsight is 20/20 and that it's easy to point fingers. It's easy to blame the rescuer, but don't let yourself do it. It's the easy way out. The rescuer may have made a big mistake, but who set them up for that failure? Focus on the risk management system as a whole—specifically the preparedness of those involved and how it impacted the events of the day. How would the culture of your team handle this scenario?

Be Proactive, Not Reactive

A well-prepared team understands that to fully explore limitations is to identify boundaries for the future. These teams are okay with being afraid.

Are you ready? Do you feel prepared?

They are willing to train a bit beyond their comfort level—perhaps even to their failure level. They hope this minimizes the opportunity for error in the future. The key, of course, is striking a reasonable balance. And therein lies the paradox: *The positive changes we make in this world cannot occur without taking the risks that we do.* Where do we draw the line? It's not an easy answer. Training to failure could be as simple as seeing how far your team can wade out into a rushing river before the water overpowers your team and washes you out. This way, you'll know in the future when to stop your progress.

Embrace preplanning and be proactive. Train for the worst, prevent it from happening, and then hope for the best. Remain situationally aware so that you can be open to identifying risks and manage them effectively. Get the whole team trained in the appropriate skill sets. Unfortunately, many rescuers finally get trained in river rescue from a reactive standpoint rather than from a proactive standpoint. A team may respond to a difficult, sometimes tragic situation, and then realize in the aftermath that more training must occur to keep responders safe and proficient. It can be haunting to find yourself wishing you had sought out more training or practice prior to going into the field.

Go beyond simply reading this book, and get trained in a two- or three-day river rescue course. And then practice, practice, practice. Good preparation includes preplanning the response to anticipated and potential problems. It means practicing the solutions with appropriate equipment and using effective communication. It's not enough to have one annual training session, especially if you haven't performed many river rescues. Certifications may last for two years, but really your credentials expire the moment you can no longer act with confidence. Risk management is not a checklist—it is a culture.

The AMI Model

The AMI risk management assessment tool is commonly used with many outdoor programs. The version presented here is an adaptation of Charles "Reb" Gregg's original model. It stands for Analyze, Manage, and Inform. This tool can be used on a large programmatic scale to develop a new training session, or on a single skill or scouting evolution. First, analyze all the risks involved with the endeavor. Next, determine what management techniques can be employed to navigate the risks effectively. Finally, communicate with your team to inform them of the plan, and open it up to questions and suggestions.

A	Analyze	Define the risks
M	Manage	Determine the options
I	Inform	Convey the plan

Use the Analyze, Manage, Inform model when approaching new risks in your environment.

Consider introducing this model to your team on your next training exercise. Perhaps you want to facilitate a wading session and you want everyone to be able to conceptualize the functionality of the AMI model. Have a transparent planning meeting, so everyone can be exposed to your thought process as you analyze the river location in which you intend to wade. Continue to use this model regularly to evaluate new hazards and to facilitate day-to-day decision-making. The AMI for wading may look like:

- Analyze the risks: *foot entrapment, strainers, hazards, communication, technique, long swims.*
- Manage techniques: *prevention, escape strategies, effective techniques, commands and signals, downstream safety, challenge by choice.*
- Inform: *an exemplary safety briefing complete with effective questioning techniques.*

Risk Management Briefings

No matter how skilled the group—or any member of it—is, always strive to have a risk management briefing prior to interacting with rivers. Everyone needs to understand that there are hazards involved when negotiating

Risk management briefings are a vital part of any day on the river. Make sure your whole team is clear about expectations and has the opportunity to contribute.

———————— Dynamics of Risk Potential ————————

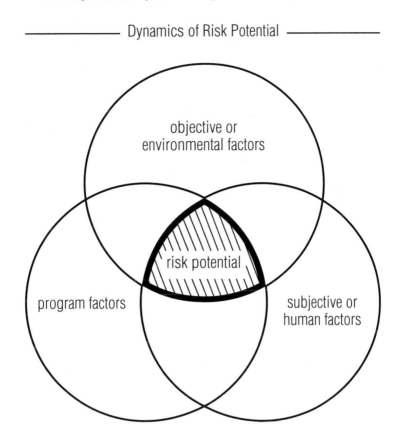

Deciding to run river trips is a serious endeavor. Think big picture, and go slow to go fast.

rivers. Managing the risks posed by these hazards takes active participation from everyone. The format of this briefing can vary, but it should inform the group of potential hazards they might encounter, risks from these hazards, and actions they can take to manage or avoid the risks. Remember, it is important for the group to be exposed to this information before encountering moving water. Review this information as needed to ensure group members have a thorough understanding of subjective and objective hazards and methods to manage these risks. Objective hazards are inherent in the environment. Subjective hazards are those we bring with us.

Subjective Hazards	Objective Hazards
Poor communication	Foot entrapment
Decision-making	Strainers
"Invincible" leadership	Rope entrapment
Complacency	Undercut banks and rocks
Distraction	Equipment failure
Overconfidence	Retentive hydraulics
Risk perception	Rejecting helical flows
Expectations and peer pressure	Long swims/flush drowning
Fatigue, stress, and performance	River traffic

Additionally, it is imperative for all group members to model behavior and decision-making that exemplifies big picture awareness and solid management of risk. If any member of the group is taking unnecessary risks and demonstrating a degree of disrespect for the power and potential of rivers, there is a great risk that other group members will emulate these actions. Establish concrete guidelines as a group, and adhere to them through leading by example.

River Safety Talk Checklist

The river safety checklist provides structure for a pre-launch talk or briefing. An example of a river safety checklist is presented below. Consider having this talk each time you return to the river. Encourage others to share their thoughts, ideas, and observations of each point to generate a stronger sense of team. Use questions to assess the understanding and comprehension of the main points. Have another team member check off items as they are introduced to ensure all information is conveyed. Take notes and modify the checklist if necessary. It should be a living document that grows along with you and your understanding of the river. Ask for different presenters of this talk over time to foster new leadership in a variety of team members.

INTRODUCTION

____ **Challenge by Choice:** Empower and encourage all to decline participation in any activity they do not want to do.

____ **Risk Management versus Safety:** Rivers are inherently unsafe places. There is real risk involved anytime you get into a river. The potential for serious injury or even death is real and must be understood and respected. It's up to all team members to contribute to the goal of managing risk.

____ **Avoid Complacency:** Maintain high awareness at all times. The more comfortable you become in the river world, the more likely you are to overlook an opportunity to prevent an injury.

____ **Medical Conditions:** Determine if medical conditions exist within the group. Introduce this as an invitation to make all aware of something such as an injured back or shoulder but also encourage private, one-on-one check-ins for more delicate cases. Stay well fed and hydrated.

____ **Emergency Plan:** Location of first aid kit, rescue supplies, cell/satellite phones, and nearest medical facility.

PPE: PERSONAL PROTECTIVE EQUIPMENT

____ **PFDs:** Styles, models, and when they are worn or removed.

____ **Helmets:** Proper fit and care requirements. Where they are worn and when they can be removed.

____ **Footwear:** Most river incidents occur on shore. Wear appropriate closed-toe footwear for river travel.

RIVER SIGNALS

____ Stop, all clear/go, go left, go right, emergency, are you OK?, eddy out.

____ Sending signals with hands versus paddles.

____ Whistle signals.

____ Importance of acknowledging and relaying signals.

SWIMMING

____ Self-rescue: Defensive versus aggressive techniques and when appropriate.

____ Keep face above water to increase spatial awareness and to hear commands from others.

____ Diving is Dangerous: Diving into the river can result in death, paralysis, brain trauma, and gasp reflex.

RIVER HAZARDS

____ Strainers, undercuts, sieves, rocks, holes, wave trains, eddies.

____ Foot entrapment.

____ Hypothermia, flush drowning, and helical flow.

THROW BAGS

____ Design, use, care, and entrapment concerns.

■ A RIVER NARRATIVE: RIGHT PLACE, RIGHT TIME

By Les Bechdel

We were a group of kayak instructors from the Nantahala Outdoor Center. It was 1979, and we were taking a busman's holiday to run the Class IV Gauley River in West Virginia. After a long summer of raft guiding and teaching kayaking classes, we were ready to cut loose and play hard. At NOC, we prided ourselves in keeping safety in the forefront of our minds whenever were working on the water. Somehow on that fall day, we were less than professional.

As we unloaded our boats below the Summersville Dam, no one discussed paddling as a group with a designated lead and sweep boat. No one discussed which rapids should be scouted. It became a frenzied race to get on the water and start surfing it up. Psychologically, I think, we were relieved not to have to worry about any students and excited to focus on fun for ourselves.

Most of us were pretty experienced paddlers. Margaret was the one exception. She had just started paddling that spring, but was an exceptional athlete, a quick learner with a great teaching style. Her roll wasn't bombproof, but she could hold her breath seemingly forever and was well practiced in T-rescue. The one thing Margaret lacked was experience in reading whitewater.

Our group spread out, and there were few other paddlers on the river that day. Margaret and I randomly entered Iron Ring Rapid at about the same time. I saw that she wasn't taking a good line and only then did a warning bell ring in the back of my mind. Looking downstream, I saw her get flipped in a huge hole, then roll up just in time to get hammered in a second hole. She flushed out without her paddle, tried one hand roll, and then tried wet exiting. The boat was jiggling but there was no sign of Margaret swimming.

I sprinted forward and slid my bow along her boat for her to do an T-rescue. No hands came up. I banged my bow into her boat again and still no response. Through the water I could see Margaret limply hanging upside-down, still in her boat. Pure panic. I pulled my kayak parallel to hers and reached across her hull. Using two hands I flipped her upright. Fortunately, Margaret is a slim lady and the waves gave me an unexpected assist. Her beet-red faced sucked a huge breath of air as she surfaced.

Apparently, her perimeter line had gotten buried, and the skirt was so tight she couldn't force her way out of her kayak. Later, in camp, she confessed that she had just about given up, then, in her words, "the hand of God pulled me up." I don't know if she was the first to coin that phrase, but it aptly describes a valuable tool for mid-river rescues. In hindsight, I do know that I should have been leading her—not following her—through Iron Ring.

A few years later, I started drafting a book about river rescue and realized the importance of being proactive in accident prevention. We identified this "what if" process of thinking to develop a "river sense" rather than relying on sheer luck to be at the right place at the right time.

Best known for his contributions to the discipline of whitewater safety and rescue, Les Bechdel has been instrumental in developing the techniques now used by river runners and rescue personnel throughout the world. Les has taught river rescue courses throughout the world and is considered one of the leading authorities on the subject. ■

CHAPTER 3

PRINCIPLES OF RIVER RESCUE

The Principles of River Rescue

1. Embrace Principles, Avoid Absolutes
2. Keep it Simple
3. River Rescue Priorities
4. Deploy Upstream and Downstream Spotters
5. Prevent Foot and Rope Entrapment
6. Scene Awareness
7. Determine Your Acceptable Level of Risk
8. Rescue Operations

1. Embrace Principles, Avoid Absolutes

The principles of river rescue provide rescuers a solid foundation for their decision-making. The principles are always evolving, as the discipline itself

Clear communication is both very important and very challenging in a rescue situation.

31

is in a constant state of change. Consider creating your own list of principles, perhaps adopting those listed here and adding others dictated by your own experience. This should be a living document, revised on a regular basis with input from your entire team as well as others in the industry.

Every, *always*, and *never* generally don't fit well in the real world, and seldom have a place at all in the river environment. Traditionally, rescue curriculums are full of absolutes. "Never stand up in the river," for example, is an absolute that many will teach on the banks of a river. The general concept makes sense; it helps prevent foot entrapment. But how can we perform a shallow-water crossing, or wade—one of our best rescue options—if we're told never to stand up in the river? Declarative sentences are important in the rescue arena, but they need to allow for judgment and reason in the face of an ever-changing environment. A reasonable principle to follow, instead of "Never stand up in the river" is "Be deliberate when deciding to stand up in a river, especially in moving water deeper than your knees." If we never stood up in deep water, we would not be able to wade or secure ourselves in a midstream eddy. At the same time, standing can cause foot entrapments, especially when standing as a way to arrest downstream momentum. Weigh these factors deliberately. Avoid absolutes and focus on principles. Granted, if we never used absolutes that would also be . . . well, absolute. Absolutes can be useful, but be careful with their placement, and use the words intentionally and practically.

Not only do absolutes fail to fit all scenarios, but they also discourage development of judgment. Absolutes rob rescuers of their ability to think. Empower one another to develop judgment and decision-making; these are the foundations of the leadership qualities we want our rescuers to have.

PRINCIPLES ALLOW FOR FLEXIBILITY AND CREATIVITY

Taking form in the 1970s, river rescue is a relatively new formal discipline. There are many skills you need to master, but being overly traditional in your approach could minimize your ability to be creative and allow for new, innovative solutions. Avoid narrow-mindedness and encourage all group members, regardless of experience level, to offer potential solutions. Rescue principles are guidelines, not rules. They are tools to help shape and guide our thinking, not limit its capacity. Try to spend more energy understanding one another's point of view when new ideas are generated, rather than immediately arguing about what is right or wrong. If you are discussing rescue and expanding your solution-oriented think tank, then you are successfully preplanning and facilitating the growth of a stronger team.

There is more than one way to get the job done. Avoid lengthy debates on the riverbank about which is the very best option and simply choose one that will work. If it falls short, be ready to implement the next idea. When seconds count, it's time to move toward action, not aggressively argue for your ideas. Discuss concepts efficiently, agree on a plan, and go get your patient.

2. Keep it Simple: Use High-Probability Solutions

Try not to blindly rely on mechanical devices and systems. We can often find ourselves with plenty of available gear, and the temptation is to use it all. The more gear you incorporate, the more time ticks off the clock, the more that can go wrong, and the more likely it'll be a body recovery rather than a patient rescue. Swiftwater teams that excel at rescue, not just recovery, are the ones that can arrive on scene and quickly deploy simple solutions with high levels of proficiency. Emphasize the fundamentals as your go-to responses: wading, strong swims, and throw bags. Try the lowest risk methods first, while higher risk alternatives are being set up.

3. River Rescue Priorities

1. Rescuer Safety
2. Group Safety
3. Patient Rescue
4. Victim Recovery
5. Equipment Recovery

RESCUER SAFETY

The first priority in all rescue situations should be the personal safety of the rescuers. Blindly and recklessly attempting to assist or save a person or piece of equipment can often add another patient to the mix. Not only is this tragic, but it adds to the operational costs of the first rescue. All too often, swiftwater incidents are reported in which would-be rescuers quickly become patients themselves after hastily rushing into the river environment. Rescuers must take a deep breath and conduct a solid scene size-up (see page 43), and then make sure they are using appropriate personal protective equipment (PPE), as described in Chapter 5.

GROUP SAFETY

The second priority is your group's safety. Back each other up, and keep people calm, cool, collected, and rational. Before succumbing to tunnel vision when responding to a person in distress, make sure the rest of your group is out of harm's way. Avoid having multiple patients in your scenario by getting the rest of the group into a safer location. Be sure their PPE is on and fastened correctly. Look for helmet straps to be buckled, PFDs tightened correctly, dry suit zippers fully closed, and shoes secured on their feet.

PATIENT RESCUE AND VICTIM RECOVERY

The third priority, after stabilizing self and group, is to rescue the patient. Rescue versus recovery is a difficult, but extremely important, distinction to make in this environment, and it is the difference between a patient and a victim. Generally speaking, any person in the river that is still a candidate for a live rescue could be referred to as a patient. Anyone who has been heads-down (airway submersed) for more than two hours could be considered unable to be saved and therefore referred to as a victim or a recovery. In some cases, rescue teams will consider it a recovery after only half an hour. Regardless of terminology, the underlying concern here is that making hasty, aggressive, uncalculated rescue attempts on a lifeless body is arguably reckless. While no one wants a body to remain in the river any longer than is necessary, it is important that extrication be from a low-risk approach. Thus, victim recovery is the fourth priority in river rescue, after self, group, and all patients are taken care of.

EQUIPMENT RECOVERY

We don't rescue gear, we recover it. The fifth priority is equipment and gear recovery. A lost oar, throw bag, or boat is trivial compared to a life. Recovery of gear and equipment should only be attempted if the risk to group members is low. Rescuers on scene need to remind one another that equipment recovery is the lowest priority and should only be attempted with a well thought-out plan.

PATIENT VERSUS BODY

One of the toughest calls a river rescuer can make is shifting phases between a rescue and a recovery. Is this person a viable patient or an expired victim? It's beneficial to be familiar with specialized considerations that can come into play when making this determination. Two significant factors for consideration in this decision are water temperature and clarity as well as the aeration of the water itself. Both of these concepts are further explored below.

Cold Water Submersion

The term immersion refers to a patient in the water and able to breathe easily. Submersion, however, refers to a patient under the water and unable to breathe.

People have been submerged in cold water for as long as sixty-six minutes and survived. When they were pulled from the water, they had no pulse and were clinically dead. Fortunately their rescuers initiated effective, well-practiced CPR immediately and kept it going all the way to the hospital—in some cases, for over ninety minutes. At the hospital, the patient's blood was

Immersion. Patient in the water and able to breathe easily.

Submersion. Patient underwater and unable to breathe.

pumped into an external machine where it was warmed and oxygenated before it was re-introduced into the body and the cardiovascular system was restarted. Contributing factors to the preservation of their bodies include the rapid cooling of their body and specifically of their brain. Additionally:

- the colder the water, the better.
- the clearer the water, the better.
- the briefer the submersion, the better.
- the sooner CPR begins, the better.

Such success stories are few and far between, though, and anytime anyone goes head-down under water, we need to prepare ourselves for a fatal outcome. We can still give them our best attempt at a rescue and hope that the effects of cold water work in their favor.

If it was a witnessed submersion in cold water, rescue efforts could be attempted for one to two hours before shifting into recovery mode. The presence of sediment in the water can shorten that window, because of the respiratory complications sediment causes when inhaled. If we've had even a few cases of people surviving after an hour of submersion, then perhaps it's worth it to attempt resuscitation of any submersion patient, particularly in cold, clear water. It's important to maintain rescue priorities, however, and cease rescue attempts if rescuers get too tired, cold, or stressed.

Solid, Hard Water or Aerated, Soft Water

Another distinction to make when identifying a patient versus a victim is whether the person is truly underwater. Just because water passes over her doesn't necessarily mean she can't breathe. When a patient goes head-down, study the water passing over her. Is it smooth, thick water or is it a bubbly flume of aerated water? Is she facing upstream, where getting any kind of breath would be nearly impossible, or is she facing downstream, where her head can create a pocket of air that might allow her to breathe?

4. Deploy Upstream and Downstream Spotters

Avoid tunnel vision by using upstream spotters to help identify and communicate to others about any debris or other boaters coming downstream into the rescue scene. If the team is unprepared for a floating tree or raft that comes sweeping into a rescue scene, tragedy could result.

Remind one another that the rescue is occurring in an active avalanche, and that people and gear may wash out and head downstream. Position spotters downstream, below the rescue, to attempt to serve as a "catcher's mitt." Ideally, you have enough personnel on scene to send a team of three rescuers downstream with throw bags and type V rescue PFDs, so that a tethered rescue swimmer can be set up to catch any unresponsive patients that wash their way. Long sticks or paddles can also be used as tools to help retrieve swimmers from the river.

5. Prevent Foot and Rope Entrapment

Every river has debris on the bottom that can cause entrapment. Rescuers unfamiliar with this threat may be tempted to stop their undesired downstream progress as a swimmer by standing up. This is a natural reaction to

NOLS instructors practicing foot entrapment rescues on the Yampa River, Colorado.

arrest one's fall, but standing up in moving water deeper than your knee could have life-threatening consequences. Foot entrapments are very dangerous, and it often requires a great deal of good luck to effect a rescue; they often result in recoveries rather than rescues. Beginners often underestimate the power of the river.

Educate your team about the danger, and teach them not to arrest their downstream progress by standing in moving water deeper than their knees, or, more simply, "Don't put your feet down when moving downstream."

Entrapped victims often flail wildly, expending all their energy in a matter of seconds. If your foot becomes trapped, try to find a secure, static position in which you can breathe. Even with a full curtain of water pouring over your head, you may still be able to position your face so you are able to breathe. Discover and create ways to prop yourself up to breathe without becoming exhausted. Try placing your arms straight, with locked elbows, on your knee to prop your upper body in a stable position. If this doesn't work, try swimming to the surface for air, then holding your breath and going face down again until another breath is needed. This may buy you a little more time and won't use up your energy and oxygen as quickly as flailing will.

ROPE ENTRAPMENT
Do not tie in to a rope or wrap it around your hands in either on-shore or in-water rescues. Many rescuers have died or been seriously injured by tying a rope around themselves or through their PFDs. Even a single wrap

around the hand to get better purchase on the rope can easily become a disaster in the river environment. You need to be able to end your connection with a rope quickly and become free of it in an instant. This is one reason every rescuer should consider carrying two knives: one that is readily available on the outside of the PFD and a second collapsible backup knife inside a PFD pocket. If a rescue swimmer needs to be directly attached to a rope, use specialized equipment, such as a Type V rescue PFD with releasable harness system.

6. Scene Awareness

Scene awareness is a critical leadership skill that includes the following concepts:

Vigilance. Keep careful watch for possible danger. Situational awareness is the ability to pay attention and notice what is happening around you. This is the leadership skill of vision. Pause after the initial assessment. Look around. Check again for hazards. Look at your people, the patient, and the scene. Avoid tunnel vision, and see the big picture by looking down on the scene from a bird's eye view. Take a look through the scene at eye level and from all angles, take another deep breath, and make a plan.

Rescuer tone. The terrain that we negotiate can be far more dangerous if our tone is inappropriate. Take shallow-water crossing, or wading, for example. Wading is an excellent technique for fast, safe, and simple access to a head-down patient, but if you are careless with your tone, you could lose your footing, wipe out, swim 100 yards downstream, and miss the window of opportunity for rescuing a viable patient. Go slow to go fast. Avoid distraction. Have appropriate urgency and focus, and maintain that focus in high and low workloads.

Task management. You must establish clear expectations and sequences for tasks, and allow for those tasks to be completed before moving on. "First we will build the anchors and mechanical advantage systems, then we can expend energy extricating the boat." Again, go slow to go fast. If you rush through your steps in the pursuit of efficiency, you waste time if the proper sequence is lost. Splint the leg first, then transport back to the river bank. Slow is smooth, smooth is fast.

Manage work overload and fatigue. You need to plan for rest and plan on fatigue. Since the Incident Coordinator is primarily hands off the rescue itself, she should be identifying when to "Call Stop" and have folks rest, particularly if there is a shift in phases between rescue and recovery. Foster and nurture a culture of self-awareness. Be aware of both internal and external limitations. In training, go beyond your comfort zone so these limitations are better known to you and to your peers.

Prepare for contingencies. PACE planning is an acronym standing for having a: **P**rimary plan, **A**lternate plan, **C**ontingency plan, and an **E**mergency plan. Essentially this is having Plan A, Plan B, Plan C, and not putting all your eggs in one basket. The trick is to anticipate where any one of your plans may fall short, and be ready to implement an alternative.

Tolerance for adversity. Spreading calm is essential on rescue scenes. Stress and emotion are inherent in challenging situations. This is especially true when the patient is someone you know and care about. How you manage these overwhelming feelings is unique to everyone, and it often reveals your true colors when operating under pressure. Regardless of what you may be experiencing internally, do your best to continue to spread calm. It's OK to be scared and uncertain of your situation, but keep that fear in check, and use it as a tool. Be encouraging, courteous, and positive with one another.

Tolerance for uncertainty. Moving forward with planning during a river rescue means accepting that we don't know if it will work or not. Identify the probabilities of your proposal, choose an effective option, and give it a try. Be prepared for a wide range of outcomes, including ones you may not have anticipated. Step back, take a deep breath, and implement your contingency plan—while creating yet another.

7. Determine Your Acceptable Level of Risk

The more time you spend training and playing in whitewater, the easier it becomes to determine the best course of action for rescue solutions. Ultimately, you must weigh the pros and cons of an idea, and the quicker you can do this, the sooner the patient can be stabilized. A risk versus benefit analysis must be performed, based on your team's proven abilities. These educated guesses should be decisions informed by evidence based on previous attempts in similar terrain. You must decide whether the risk to yourself and your group is worth taking, based on the probability of a successful rescue. Run through your rescue options and determine which ones offer the most promise for an efficient outcome. Rank these options based on the level of risk they impose to all on scene, then determine your acceptable level of risk, and begin your rescue. Running through this exercise also generates contingency planning, so you can initiate your next option should the first attempt fall short of success. It sometimes makes sense to try an option a couple of times before moving on to the next idea. Learn from the first attempt, and try to improve upon it before determining it invalid. But remember, historically there is a direct connection between heightened emotions and rescuer fatalities. Call stop on all rescue activities if it appears decisions are based purely on emotion.

RESCUE OPTIONS

It's critical that rescue personnel understand the basic categories of rescue techniques and the risks involved to both patient and rescue team. Determining the probability of these options succeeding has everything to do with the difficulty of the terrain and the proven ability of the individual rescuer making the attempt; the more times a rescuer has practiced a technique, the more viable it becomes.

DON'T OPERATE BEYOND YOUR ACCEPTABLE LEVEL OF RISK

Deciding what to do in a rescue situation requires gut instinct based on real experience in similar situations. Hours of training and practice are necessary to determine your acceptable level of risk. This should be the ultimate goal in any training session, and it must be understood that individuals will have their own, unique determination of what is acceptable. Deciding whether to wade, throw, paddle, or swim out to a patient can only be done reasonably and rationally if that skill has been practiced several times before.

Determine what you are capable of and what level of risk you are willing to assume. Account for this with plenty of recent practice. Your acceptable level of risk for swimming a rapid isn't based on how well you swam whitewater two years ago; it's based on how well you can do it today. The

To better determine your acceptable level of risk, test your swiftwater swimming skills frequently.

Signal	Patients in the water sometimes take on a nearly catatonic mental state and appear almost uninterested in self-rescue. Often they simply need coaching and encouragement. Snap them out of this dream state with a well-placed whistle blast and direct command. This should almost always happen, regardless of what comes next. Often just quickly shouting to the patient, "Swim this way!" with a clear hand signal will have a dramatic effect. Communicating directly and immediately with the patient increases the potential for a positive outcome. This is the lowest-risk option to the rescuer and patient since no one new is being introduced into the river, nor is any equipment that could pose an entrapment threat or injury.
Extend	When effective, consider reaching out with a stick, paddle, or object to pull the patient back to shore. This is another lower-risk option to rescuers since they are still on shore and not in the moving water. Be sure to have solid footing and, when possible, recruit a backup to secure the primary rescuer and make sure he does not fall in while retrieving the patient.
Wade	Wading is sometimes a fast, simple option when trying to access a specific point in the river, when the depth and current allow for it. Depending on the technique and number of rescuers used, it may not require any equipment at all. It is a higher-risk option since rescuers are not only entering the water, but are exposing themselves to both foot entrapment and unintended swimming.
Throw	Throw ropes are common in rescue situations, and can be a simple option for a well-practiced rescuer. Throwing a rope or flotation device directly to the swimmer means the rescuer can stay on shore, but it does introduce entrapment potential.
Boat	Using a boat to access a patient can be a simple option if it is driven by an advanced operator. It could also be achieved by belaying a boat on a tether to a precise location in the river. Even though the rescuers are now on the water itself, this can still sometimes be less risky and have higher probability of success than throwing a rope. It can also be disastrous if operators are oblivious to their actual ability or the severity of hazards in the area.
Swim	Entering the river as a rescue swimmer to retrieve a patient is one of the riskiest options for consideration. This can be done with or without a tether. Adding a fixed line onto the rescuer, even on a releasable harness makes this significantly more dangerous than going without. It may be that some form of a rescue swim is the simplest and easiest option for a high-probability rescue.

longer it's been since you've practiced a skill, the less legitimacy you have for proposing a true sense of what is and isn't acceptable risk. Practice often. Practice intentionally. And practice beyond your comfort zone, to your failure point. Then you can make informed decisions based on your own determinations of present limitations and abilities.

Experts use recognition-primed decisions. They recognize a situation as typical of a class of situations, they mentally test a response, and then they act by recognizing key features. Experts can misperceive risks just like anybody else, but they are ideally operating within their acceptable levels of risk. They have a strong sense of what they can and cannot do. They should know when to say "No" and when to say "It's worth a try given the present risk to me and to the patient." Experts should know that to consider an option is to fully envision the likelihood and consequences of both a successful and failed attempt.

RIVERS ARE CONSISTENTLY UNDERESTIMATED, ACTIVE AVALANCHES

Continue to remind yourself that every river is a constant avalanche. It's a moving debris fan that you actively negotiate. Rivers are mountains falling down right in front of you. Even the seemingly benign sections of moving water should be taken very seriously. Many river incidents and rescue

If you swim unexpectedly, catching an eddy and hauling out on the rock that caused it can offer an opportunity to rest and assess next steps.

blunders occur on relatively mild sections of river, just flat water or Class I–III. Anytime we step into a rescue scenario we need to register that it could be the last thing we do.

EVERY RAPID IS A BRAND NEW RAPID

The avalanche continues to carve and sculpt the river into new formations and features every day. Approach rapids like it is your first time running them or responding to them. Regardless of how many times you've established safety for a particular rapid, always be open to new solutions. The more times you've run a rapid, the more legitimate experience you've gained. But your lens can lose focus, and your brain may assume everything is the same as last time. Team members new to the rapid bring tremendous value and should be asked for their viewpoint of the rapid and its hazards. Inquire what solutions they would consider in this location, and embrace it as an excellent opportunity for fresh perspective.

8. Rescue Operations

SIZE UP THE SCENE

People want to help one another. It is a wonderful characteristic of the human species that we will rush to help those in need. Learning to harness this energy is critical for all rescuers approaching the river. If you don't, you could easily become an additional patient in a real scenario. The foundation of sound decision-making is having a solid understanding of your present situation. Consider the following elements before rushing into a scene to help:

1. Danger
2. Mechanism of incident
3. Personal protective equipment
4. Number of patients
5. Contingencies
6. Acceptable level of risk

- **Danger.** Is there a risk of physical harm to you, fellow responders, bystanders, and the patient? How can that risk be minimized? If it's not safe to approach, then don't.
- **Mechanism of incident (MOI).** What happened or is happening? Where was the patient last seen? What are the environmental hazards that could have contributed to the injury?
- **Personal protective equipment (PPE).** Make sure you are wearing appropriate rescue equipment prior to engaging: rescue PFD, water sports helmet, closed-toe footwear, thermal protection, knife,

When resources allow, consider having an Incident Coordinator on scene to facilitate big-picture operations and contingency planning.

whistle, etc. Note that firefighting gear is not appropriate for swift-water rescue. The brightly colored, fire-retardant, full-body suits worn by firefighters is called turnout gear. Firefighters' turnouts can quickly fill with water, and fire helmets have a large brim that can torque the head uncontrollably in the current.

- **Number of patients.** Be aware that other patients may exist beyond the obvious one screaming in front of you.
- **Contingencies.** Is this a rescue or a recovery? What resources (people or equipment) do you have on hand that could affect the outcome? Consider what sequence of events is most likely to happen and how the presence or absence of rescuer action may affect those events. For example, one contingency may be that if the patient is freed from her midstream entrapment prematurely, she could float right into the strainer 50 yards downstream. Therefore, it would make sense to station a rescuer with a throw bag far above that strainer in case this contingency becomes a reality.
- **Acceptable level of risk.** What is the worst-case scenario of failing in your attempted rescue option? Would this result in serious injury or death to you as the rescuer? To others on scene? When was the last time you tried what you are about to do, and how proficient were you in this type of terrain? Are you making a calculated or heroic decision? Would others with your same abilities make the same decision in this situation?

Establishing Incident Command

Whenever resources allow, there should be an Incident Commander or Incident Coordinator (IC) who oversees the rescue operations. Ideally, the IC maintains big-picture awareness and effective communication by staying out of the actual rescue work and patient care. ICs are attempting to look down on the situation from above and direct traffic while constantly reassessing probabilities and contingencies. They are ready to call a halt when risk management concerns arise. ICs excel at directive leadership while also being courteous, spreading calm, and instilling confidence in others. They should be prioritizing patients, coordinating resources, delegating tasks, and making evacuation priority decisions. Discuss with your team ahead of time how this role will be assigned and what it entails in order to initiate an efficient rescue when it really matters. Communication is essential to effective management.

PLAN OF OPERATION

Using the information compiled from the scene size-up, decisions can be made, and a plan can be formed. Think ahead and create multiple plans because one of the possibilities may spoil your primary attack plan. In other words, avoid putting all your eggs in one basket. Instead, plan for the worst and hope for the best. Finally, be sure to have an efficient on-scene safety

Effective and intentional communication is critical in rescue scenarios.

briefing outlining organization and management. Additional tools that are helpful for making an effective plan include:

- **STOP—Sit, Think, Observe, Plan.** Be comfortable with the silence and lack of activity as you stop and think about the situation. This is something leaders often struggle with, as they feel their action and prowess must occupy all space and time. Spread calm, and allow yourself to think through the process before leaping into a potentially dangerous situation.
- **PACE Planning—Primary, Alternative, Contingency, Emergency Plans.** Re-evaluate your backup plans on a regular basis. Whether you call it PACE planning or simply establishing Plan A, Plan B, and Plan C, it's imperative that your plans include multiple options and steps toward setting each one up from the beginning.
- **Decision-making.** When building your plan, think about looking down on the rescue scene from a vantage point high above. Much like a sports coach making a game plan, this is where you establish the Xs and Os of both your offensive and defensive strategies.
- **Sense-making.** After applying the decision-making tool above, look through the scenario standing at water level to anticipate how everyone will make sense of things as they unfold. Remember, assessing a rapid from an elevated position is deceiving. The rapid is often dramatically more difficult than it appears from above.

River Rescue Zones

Managing risk means managing people. An effective way to achieve this goal is to identify and honor boundaries. Preplanning sessions should include defining the areas of the river where different personnel can position themselves during a river rescue, based on their skill levels and personal protective equipment. The goal of creating these boundaries is to minimize the risk of additional patients or challenges and to allow for rescue operations to continue without unnecessary distraction.

THE GREEN ZONE
Anyone not actively participating in the rescue should remain in the Green Zone. This is also called the Cold Zone. This is where EMS, fire, SAR, and law enforcement professionals can stage while the rescue is conducted. This is also the appropriate place for beginner river runners, clients, bystanders, and members of the media. Using rope or flagging tape can be helpful to clearly identify the Green Zone boundary. Anyone positioned in this zone needs to understand its purpose; when resources allow, have a designated leader of this zone to direct personnel and bystanders. No one should enter

the Red or Yellow zones unless they have been invited and are wearing appropriate PPE.

THE YELLOW ZONE

Depending on the topography of the riverbank, the Yellow Zone is comprised of the area within 10 to 30 feet of the water itself. This is also sometimes referred to as the Warm Zone. Anyone operating in this area should have full river PPE on and be prepared for an unintentional swim or slip and fall on rocks. Many river injuries occur on the shoreline. PFDs and helmets offer necessary protection, even on dry land. Yellow Zone operators should have sixteen to twenty-four hours of river rescue education.

THE RED ZONE

The Red Zone, also known as the Hot Zone, is the area of the river itself, and is defined by the riverbanks. Personnel operating in this zone should have complete river PPE and at least sixteen to twenty-four hours of river rescue training. Red Zone operators ideally will have considerable river experience and be able to self-rescue by aggressively swimming should they get unintentionally swept away in the current. It is important that those operating in the Red Zone have a firm grasp of their own acceptable levels of risk.

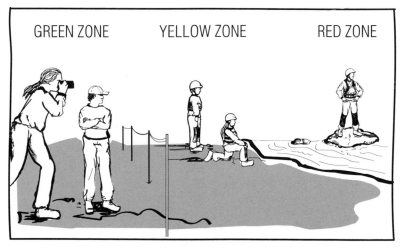

The green zone should be clearly marked area by the incident coordinator to indicate where bystanders and anyone without proper river PPE can stand. Rescuers in the designated yellow zone should be wearing full river PPE and be ready to assist. Personnel in the red zone, or actively working within the river itself, should be experienced river rescue technicians.

Search and Rescue Basics

Numerous textbooks, courses, and curriculums exist today that examine the discipline of search and rescue (SAR) in much detail. Readers interested in learning more about SAR operations are encouraged to seek out these resources for a complete picture of the necessary skills. Local agencies often manage the SAR units for their counties and ultimately oversee and dictate SAR decision-making. Some of the basics of SAR operations are outlined here, since there is often an overlap with river runner incidents and SAR teams arriving on scene.

INITIAL APPROACH

Generally, emergency medical services (EMS) and river rescuers begin their response to rescue any situation with a complete survey of the scene. search and rescue teams, as the name implies, must often find the patient before a rescue can occur. They have formal procedures to allow them to focus search efforts, and may adhere to them in river rescue situations where the location of the patient is unknown.

INTERVIEW OF SUBJECT PROFILE

To better direct search efforts, the sheriff or SAR commander will often conduct interviews with witnesses or companions of the missing person. This is usually done in a one-on-one conversation with the same interviewer from start to finish. The interviewer is often strategically alternating between open-ended and close-ended questions.

Open-ended questions may provide useless information at times, but the interviewee can be expressive and share good insight. Examples of open-ended questions are: "How was his mindset prior to his disappearance?" or "Is there anything else you think I should know?"

Close-ended questions typically only allow for one-word responses. They can be more time efficient in an interview and allow easy note taking. They can be useful for comparison with other witnesses' responses, but it's easier for the interviewee to lie, and the interviewer can miss important information if her questions aren't specific enough.

Interviewers will often use one of several acronyms to stay organized and on-track with their questioning. One common acronym used is **SWEETT**.
Subject: age, sex, medical history. This also includes:
Name—given name and preferred nickname, emergency contact information
Physical description—height, weight, eye color, and other descriptors
Clothing description—boot pattern, scent article (socks or t-shirt for dog trackers)

Effective rescue briefings require tested systems and intentional techniques by all team members.

Attitude—Would subject hide from searchers or be embarrassed? Are they happy, sad, or in trouble?

Weather: past, present, and forecasted

Experience: Does the subject have outdoor skills? Is he a boater, a NOLS graduate, a Boy Scout, or former military? Does he have river rescue training?

Equipment: What equipment did the subject have: PFD, helmet, food, dry suit?

Time: How long has subject been missing? Where was he last seen? (PLS—point last seen; LKP—last known point)

Terrain: What are the hazards: rapids, strainers, waterfalls, rugged banks, dense forest?

PHASES OF A RESCUE
The phases of a rescue can be remembered with the acronym LAST.

Locate: The first phase of a rescue is to locate the patient. This is sometimes an easy task if the patient can be seen at a fixed point in the river, and witnesses can verify there are no additional patients. Other times, a patient could be entrapped below the surface of the water, requiring careful scanning of the environment to determine her location. A patient may even be stuck below the surface on a rock that a rescuer is standing on, and the only way she will be detected is if the rescuer looks straight down through the rapidly moving water and sees bright pieces of clothing. Patients could also

Rescuers practicing swimming skills, throw bag skills, and tethered rescue swims in a Class III rapid.

be traveling in the water, requiring rescuers to give chase on land or in the water. In these cases the search could last hours or days before a rescue or recovery can be performed.

Access: After determining the number of patients and locating each of them, a decision must be made about which rescue method to use for accessing the patients. Being ready with contingency plans for accessing the patients goes a long ways toward conducting an efficient rescue, since the primary plan can sometimes fall short of success.

Stabilize: After making contact with the patient, you must stabilize her. A competent, complete rescue technician should have solid first aid skills combined with river rescue training. Basic life support measures, such as CPR and airway management, may be needed at this point. Conducting a full patient assessment in the middle of the river isn't always possible, but it should be a primary consideration when stabilizing a patient. The patient should also be provided with appropriate PPE, such as a well-fitted PFD and helmet, before continuing with extrication.

Transport: The final phase of the rescue requires transporting the patient back to shore and on to definitive care if necessary. This may be as simple as loading her into an ambulance or may require river travel to get to an access point. In extreme cases a helicopter may be dispatched and therefore a landing zone must be prepared.

■ A RIVER NARRATIVE: LITTLE HEATER

By Nate Ostis

I was being tossed around like a rag doll. Which way is up? I can't hold my breath any longer. Everything is going black. My brother is going to have to recover my body and then call our parents. I'm so scared. I don't know what to do. I don't want to die . . . but this is it.

It was June 1996 when I almost drowned while kayaking. At this point in our paddling careers, we had run this section of the West Branch of the Penobscot River in northern Maine several hundred times—just never at this high of a level before. The four of us— Sam, Hutch, my brother Jay, and I—were all best friends and guided together on this stretch of river. We'd all been through plenty of adventures together and knew each other's every move. We trusted each other's decisions and knew what to do when things went wrong. Perhaps this overall familiarity with the river and my companions is what lead to me almost losing my life.

The Penobscot typically runs around 2,600 cubic feet per second (cfs) and is considered a Class IV-V run through Ripogenus Gorge and the Cribworks. This particular spring saw tremendous amounts of rain, resulting in levels upwards of 20,000 cfs. For weeks no one touched the upper section of the river. All commercial raft trips were altered to launch 10 miles downstream where the gradient let up considerably.

One day, somewhat suddenly, the flow dropped down to 8,000 cfs. This was still an extremely high level for the narrow gorge, but much lower than we'd seen all season. We decided to take a look to see if it was worth a run in our kayaks. After scouting most of the upper section, we all felt comfortable with the decision to run Ripogenus Gorge. Although the water was enormous, it was reasonable to see the moves, which included several sneak options. The first mile slipped by successfully with us eddy-hopping most of the way. We reached the first big pool and let out a huge scream of excitement. We had made it through the Dryway and Exterminator. Next, we approached the Heaters, where boaters can choose going to one side or the other of a massive granite block standing tall in the center of the river. Going left takes one through Big Heater, a wide-open mellow section with easy, read-and-run gradient. Going right takes one through Little Heater, a narrow 6-foot drop into a big recovery pool. The granite walls on either side of the drop extend straight upward for 60 feet making it a beautiful little spot. Either option is very reasonable at normal flows in rafts and kayaks and runs are generally fun and uneventful.

We decided to scout Little Heater and see if it was safe to run. Due to the sheer gorge walls, we were unable to get close enough for a good look. The drop was only 20 feet away from where we were standing, but we couldn't see the hole at the bottom, so we decided to paddle around Big Heater and play it safe. Sam and Hutch got back to their boats first and paddled around the island through Big Heater. My brother and I were slower getting back to our boats, as we discussed how amazing the upstream adventure had been. As I sealed

Looking downstream at the Heaters on the West Branch of the Penobscot river. Little Heater on river right, Big Heater on river left.

my spray skirt back on to my kayak, I looked downstream to the recovery pool below Little Heater to see Sam and Hutch paddling back upstream.

This is where things fell apart. As I made eye contact with Hutch 100 yards away, he raised his paddle into a vertical orientation, the signal we've always used for "All clear!" and "Go!" My interpretation of his message and the intentions of his signal turned out to be very different. I thought Hutch could now see the hole at the bottom of Little Heater, and it looked good to go. I had no doubts in his judgment. I trusted him completely. What I found out later was that Hutch was merely connecting with us in order to say, "Hey, here we are and we're OK. Are you guys OK?" Due to the extreme intensity of the day's paddle and the unusually loud thunder produced through the gorge walls from the increased flow, Hutch was almost over-cautious in his communication. I could plainly see both him and Sam in the recovery pool and could easily recognize they were safe. I didn't consider Hutch wanting to convey to me what I could already see. Instead, without a doubt in the world, I turned to my brother, "Hutch says it looks clean, I'll see you at the bottom."

Jay replied, "Great, I'm right behind you. Have fun."

Reaching the lip of the drop I had run hundreds of times before, I expected to see the same thing, only on a larger scale. Instead, I knew immediately I was in trouble. Below me was a huge, thrashing toilet bowl hydraulic with a boil line 20 feet downstream. The river is only about 8 feet wide through this section, and the hole was wall-to-wall. I got hammered. Cartwheels, back enders, window shades, and flailing braces led to me pulling my skirt and swimming for it. No dice. This hole had zero interest in letting me go. Downtime in between recirculations averaged around seven to ten seconds. I remember clawing with my fingers at the gorge walls underwater, desperate for any kind of purchase. I tried swimming deeper to find exit currents and instead used up valuable energy and oxygen. I was at the complete mercy of the river.

The last time I recirculated, I gave up fighting. I didn't have anything left. I entered a dreamy, space-like black out. I remember thinking of my family and picturing my brother calling my parents. Telling them the story of my drowning and the location of my body.

Then, like a cat with a mouse, the river gods decided to let me go, as if my lesson had been learned. Sam said I erupted up out of the water up to my waist right at the boil line, completely motionless with my head limp on my shoulder, before bobbing downstream. Hutch immediately pulled me onto his deck and paddled me to shore. By the time I got there, I had come to and was answering Hutch's repeated shouts of my name. I vomited and collapsed with exhaustion.

We learned a lot that day about how quickly things can go from seemingly simple to absolutely life-threatening. No individual blame was placed in this situation. It was on all of us. We instead spent our time processing and sharing ideas about where we needed to elevate our game and how to prevent future incidents from occurring.

Nate Ostis is the author of the NOLS River Rescue Guide *and an editor of the* NOLS River Educator Notebook. *He is a senior field instructor for NOLS and the founder of Wilderness Rescue International.* ■

CHAPTER 4

EFFECTIVE COMMUNICATION

Briefings

To make sound decisions, we need accurate information and a team environment conducive to effective communication. No matter how skilled, you and your group should have a risk management briefing before going out on the river. All team members need to understand the hazards of negotiating rivers, and that managing these hazards takes active participation from everyone. The briefing should inform the group of potential hazards they might encounter and actions they can take to help manage or avoid those hazards.

Likewise, practice and demonstrate basic safety skills before going out on the water. Review this information as needed so that group members have a thorough understanding of subjective and objective hazards, and the difference between them. All group members need to be aware of the big

Discuss and plan communication expectations as part of your regular training.

picture and be able to manage risk and practice sound decision-making. If one member of the group takes unnecessary risks or shows disrespect for the power of the river, other members might follow suit. Establish concrete guidelines as a group and adhere to them through leading by example.

Too often, swiftwater rescue failures are reviewed and found to have glaring errors in understanding among team members in the briefing process. Personnel can get spread out fast, losing visibility, supervision, and the ability to communicate effectively. This is why it is so important to have an effective plan for communicating with the team. Practice swiftwater briefings. Practicing throwing ropes is essential too, but we all need to practice communicating effectively, so when real emotion comes into play, we can still manage our systems.

Effective briefings have no extra verbiage and are delivered with conviction. Use common terminology: "I need you to go build me a 3-point load distributing boatman's anchor using a double figure 8 on a bight. Be sure to have a second rescuer double check your work." Every time any team member builds an anchor or a system, it is beneficial for them to state out loud what they've just done, in as few words as possible and using terms familiar to the team. Speaking takes practice. Be simple, clear, and succinct. Brief the team again at any phase change. Brief to keep your team informed, to share information, and to state decisions and plans. Here's a simple format to consider when facilitating both briefings and debriefs:

Briefing	Debrief
1. This is our situation.	1. What was planned?
2. This is what I think we should do.	2. What actually happened?
3. This is why.	3. Why did it happen?
4. Remember these key safety considerations.	4. What can we do next time?
5. Who has questions or thoughts?	

Questioning versus Advocacy

This is perhaps one of the most challenging aspects of communication within a rescue squad. When it comes to planning within a team, generating a group consensus can be valuable before moving into action. Consensus decisions inherently have more buy-in from group members and can identify pitfalls and blind spots in plans. However, they take time to generate, and in a rescue situation, time can be a valuable resource. When participating in a group planning process, recognize there is more than one way to get the job done and that team members may want to do things differently. Before interjecting and introducing a different idea into the proposed plan, ask yourself, "Is the existing plan adequate, or do I really have something better to offer?" Put another way, "Is this a difference that makes a difference?"

Are you just proposing something different to hear yourself speak and to demonstrate your prowess, or do you actually see some gaps in risk management and efficiency? If you have a substantially better plan, speak up. That's your responsibility as a team member. But if your idea is basically the same gist with only subtle differences, your most valuable contribution to the process may be keeping it to yourself.

Even though you may want to approach the problem differently, it is sometimes better to go with the given plan and remember there is a patient that needs help. This requires a conscious effort and is another example of what ultimately contributes to a culture or risk management and a team that is effective at rescue. Differentiating between the "best" way and a "good" way isn't always necessary when seconds count. Don't let "perfect" get in the way of "good enough."

Know River Signals!

ESTABLISH A CALL STOP COMMAND

All personnel should be empowered to call STOP anytime they get a gut feeling that something isn't right or is about to go wrong. This is especially true for the novice and beginners on scene who often see things with a fresher perspective. It is sometimes the quietest voice or person with the least amount of experience that observes some of the biggest blunders we're about to make out there. Encourage and support others to speak up.

HAND SIGNALS

It can be difficult to hear on the river, especially next to rapids, so a set of nonverbal river signals has been developed using paddles or arms. When communicating using these signals, it is important to indicate you've received and understood a signal by repeating it back to the deliverer and passing it on to others who are behind you.

STOP!

Form a horizontal bar with your outstretched arms.
Potential hazard ahead. Wait for "All Clear" signal before proceeding, or scout ahead. Stop in a safe place or pull to shore as quickly as possible.
This signal can also be delivered by holding a paddle up high in a horizontal position.

All clear! Go! Come ahead! Keep coming!

One arm or paddle held vertically high above the head.
If using a paddle, the blade should be turned flat for maximum visibility.
In the absence of other directions, proceed down the center of the river.

Go this way!

To signal a preferred course through a rapid or around an obstruction, **lower the previously vertical "All Clear" by 45° toward the side of the river with the preferred route.**
Don't point toward the obstacle you wish to avoid.

Eddy out over here!

One hand rotated above the head, then pointed directly to the eddy you want them to go to.
"Eddy out in this eddy *here*." This differs from the "STOP" command, as eddying out can potentially be a more relaxed and less time-sensitive maneuver. STOP means stop everything that you are doing or stop your boat however you can as soon as you can.

(continued)

Help! Emergency! I need your eyes and/or your assistance!

Give three long blasts on a whistle while waving a paddle, helmet, or life vest over your head.
Assist the signaler as quickly as possible and consider the need for a first aid kit before reaching them.
If a whistle is not available, use the visual signal alone.
TIP: A whistle can be carried on a plastic lanyard attached to your PFD.

Are you OK?

Point at the person with one arm and pat your head with the other. This is the signal asking if you are OK. This signal was adopted from the scuba industry, where verbal communication is near impossible. This signal is often used as the question, "Are you OK?" Respond by placing your hand on your head to indicate that you are okay. If you are not okay, respond with a help signal or simply shake your head "No."

It may be that you just took an unexpected swim and are now on the opposite side of the river, cold, frustrated, and tired. You may not be okay with what just happened but are uninjured and just need a brief rest. In this case you would still reply, "I'm OK." This should be understood as you don't need immediate attention. The "No" signal should be reserved exclusively for indicating that a true emergency or injury is in play.

Some river runners use this interchangeably with the "Go" or "All Clear" signal. It's advisable to have one dedicated signal for asking after one's well-being, and for many professionals, it is the "Are you OK?" signal.

WHISTLE SIGNALS

Ideally everyone on a river trip or on a river rescue scene has a whistle. (The Fox 40 whistle continues to be the leading product on the market.) Any concerns about misuse of the whistle can be easily overcome with simple instruction. A sharp whistle blast can be heard, even over the noise of whitewater, and is much more effective than trying to yell over and over. While in some specialized situations it can helpful to have a variety of whistle blast signals, generally it is best to keep things simple. Whistles should only be used when necessary so they are taken seriously when they are heard. A good system to follow is:

One whistle blast means, "Attention! I need your eyes so I can give you hand signals."

Multiple blasts (often in groups of three) mean "Emergency!"

RADIO COMMUNICATIONS

Handheld radios can be a valuable resource, but they require disciplined and intentional communication. This takes practice, and without familiarity with this tool, it is often best not to use it. Waterproof models exist, but it's important not to exceed their rated limits. Waterproof cases are another option, but these can sometimes decrease functionality.

Acknowledging, Understanding, and Clarifying Roles

Military personnel will often use the phrase HUAA during briefings to acknowledge that the plan is understood. HUAA stands for **H**eard, **U**nderstood, **A**nd **A**cknowledged. For some this is a bit too regimented, and they prefer a simple call of "Clear?" by the IC and "Clear" in reply by the team. The important point here is that the messages delivered are heard and understood. Have a simple and efficient way of determining this.

Another step that can really catch misunderstandings before they develop into mishaps is to have a team member summarize the plan after the IC has delivered it. How do we know what our team knows unless we account for it? If we simply ask, "Everyone got it?" we're not assessing the effectiveness of our briefing. Taking the extra minute to have someone else give a synopsis can help catch glaring errors in communication and vision. Minimize assumptions and seek clarity.

Staying Alert on the River

The river environment is full of naturally occurring objective hazards as well as subjective hazards introduced by humans. Understanding the concept of objective and subjective hazards can increase your awareness and your ability to stay alert on the river. Objective hazards are those aspects of the natural world and its forces that present risks. In the river environment they include river features such as rocks, undercuts, strainers, and hydraulics. Subjective hazards are factors such as the characteristics, personalities and behaviors of people, and they include fatigue, physical strength, and perception. In a rescue situation, a common subjective hazard is a breakdown in communication, which can pose a unique challenge in a

Downstream spotters must be ready to act at a moment's notice and wearing appropriate PPE.

dynamic river environment. Incidents generally happen when an objective hazard overlaps with a subjective hazard, like when someone, tired at the end of a long day, takes a swim in a gnarly rapid. The forces of a river's moving water compound the threat to life as a result of a mishap. Group members need to be clear about expectations. Something as simple as keeping everyone informed of the daily plan on the river or in which order boats will run a specific rapid is important.

Stay aware of your group and gear while you are on, in, or around rivers. The boat in front of you might pull over because they see a potential hazard downstream. If you have been paying attention, you'll see them and can signal the boats behind you. Likewise, looking back upriver is important because a boat behind you may be signaling "Emergency!" Be aware of where other people in your group are.

Some people describe trip awareness as being aware of the trip in front of them, the trip behind them, and where they fit into the trip. Rivers with long, calm stretches can breed complacency in boaters, but you need to keep alert at all times on the river, not just while running rapids. Group management includes maintaining reasonable communication between boats, spacing boats properly for running rapids—so you are close enough to back each other up but not so close that you get in each other's way—and placing specific boats in lead and sweep positions. (For example, you might have your friend in a highly maneuverable cataraft drop the rapid and eddy in below the rapid as a spotter. Her job is to help anyone who swims the rapid or has any other problem, and she needs to be immediately beneath the rapid, ready to row out and help a swimmer. You might have the first aid kit, pulleys, and certified first aid guru go last in the sweep boat.) It is fine if group management strategies change, as long as it's done actively and deliberately. Develop basic self-discipline at the team level and many major river problems will remain just minor near-misses.

■ A RIVER NARRATIVE: SWIM BEERS

By KT Smith

The game had one rule, and it was simple: If you fell out of your boat, you had to buy everybody who worked that day, bus drivers and office staff included, one beverage of their choice. An inadvertent swim on a busy day meant you'd spend considerably more money than you made that day. And though over the years there was some debate over the precise definition of "fell out of your boat," for the most part, the game and its rule remained unchallenged. Usually the beverage was a beer, but the game was never about drinking. It was fun and funny as you'd expect, but it was also more than that.

The game was a measure of the pride we took in guiding. Many companies officially condemn "raft 'em up" guiding—intentional flips, dump-trucks, etc.—while in reality turning a blind eye. For us, though, that sentiment actually lived within the culture of the guides. We esteemed going big with style, and style to us meant an upright boat at the bottom of each rapid. Good-natured heckling was a powerful tool that kept us striving to do better. We held each other to high standards. The game reinforced that.

I've guided at many other companies with guides that were equally skilled, but where was something lacking—an atmosphere of trust. The river is dynamic, and even the best guides make mistakes. At our company, it was part of our culture to be proactive. I knew the guides on the water with me were tuned in. They knew how many guests I had in my boat, if they were having fun, and if they were an effective team. We knew when a guide was having an off day or needed closer safety because it mattered to us to pay attention. On days when I swam, the game allowed me to say thank you to the family of people that worked hard to have my back.

Over time I came to realize that it wasn't just a game, it was how we lived. We didn't punch our timecard at the end of the day and go home. When the trip was put away, we gathered in the parking lot. Swim beers, if there were any, got handed out and then a truly remarkable thing would happen: the stories. We told stories, and we learned from each other. We learned about rapids and features, about prepping our crews with good information. We learned pitfalls to look out for like complacency, ego, and eagerness to please. We learned humility and responsibility. We learned to take care of the people around us and to trust them to do the same. We shared our experiences. The stories told in that parking lot made me a better and more conscientious boater than any other aspect of my training or career. And I owe that in large part to the game and to the way we played it.

KT Smith has worked professionally in rivers across the globe since the late 1990s. Her home rivers are the New and the Gauley in West Virginia. She teaches in the white-water, backpacking, and wilderness medicine programs for NOLS. She was a guide for the USA women's whitewater rafting team, and she teaches swiftwater rescue. ■

CHAPTER 5

APPROPRIATE RIVER EQUIPMENT

Personal Protective Equipment: The Essentials for Everyone

Swiftwater rescue requires immediate response and reliable equipment, training, and technique. Efficiency is important, and having the right equipment can make the difference when every second counts. It is important to understand what equipment is essential for all individual personnel in the river before moving on to bigger group gear considerations. The essential gear for each individual is listed below, followed by detailed explanations:

1. Helmet
2. Type V rescue personal flotation device (PFD)
3. Rescue knives (2)
4. Locking carabiners (4)
5. Micro-trauma shears
6. Thermal protection and proper clothing
7. Rescue belt (15' of 1" webbing)
8. Closed-toe shoes
9. Rescue saw
10. High-quality throw bag
11. Prusiks (2)
12. Pulleys (3)

Appropriate safety gear is as much a requirement for recreating in whitewater as a boat.

HELMET

In general, whenever a PFD is being used, a well-fitting helmet should be considered, especially in a rescue scenario or when paddling anything harder than a Class II rapid. The type of craft you are paddling is a factor in determining when exactly to put the helmet on, but in a whitewater setting, helmets should always be readily accessible. The helmet should be securely fastened for a snug, comfortable fit. Other features to consider when selecting a helmet include:

- Y-straps: Chin straps with Y-formation attachment points on the helmet are designed to prevent the helmet from rocking back on the head and exposing the forehead. In the Y-formation, the chin strap anchors to two points on both sides of the helmet, one point slightly behind the ear and the other slightly in front of the ear. Note, however, that Y-straps must be adjusted properly to protect the head; the chin strap can feel tightly fitted when in fact one leg or the other of the Y is still quite loose. A loose leg can allow a helmet to rock and expose parts of the skull. Ensure everyone in your group knows how to adjust their helmets so that both legs of each Y are under equal tension. Increase awareness in your group about this critical aspect of the helmet so everyone knows how to critique others.

WRSI

SHRED
READY
HELMETS

- Brims: Some helmets have no brims while others have brims that extend as far as the classic baseball cap. Although often thought of as a feature for the sun or for style, these brims also provide a safety feature for a foot-entrapped patient. The brim encourages the water to wash away from the face in a partial submersion incident, creating a plume with a hidden air pocket right in front of the patient's airway.
- Coverage: Helmet selection should be an intentional decision, after careful consideration of the pros and cons. Recognize the trade-offs of

different features. For example, some find ear coverage too hot and say it interferes with their hearing. But smashing your exposed ear on a rock could result in a life-altering injury. Ear coverage also protects your ears from the sun. It minimizes excessive cold water entering the ear canal, which can result in "surfer's ear" or loss of hearing from inner ear growths that occur with chronic cold water exposure.

• Ratchet systems: Many newer designs have fastening systems that help secure the helmet to your skull and allow for greater adjustability when seasonal haircuts and thermal skull caps can change the desired fit. They also allow for more users to swap out the same gear sets with minimal adjustments.

BODY ARMOR

River rescue in shallow rivers can be rough on your body and result in significant bumps and bruises, particularly if there are a lot of manmade elements in the river, such as concrete, rebar, and blasted rock from road construction. Slippery surfaces covered with slimy algae result in many falls and injuries along the shoreline. If you expect to go swimming, you need to be ready to get banged up. Adding elbow pads, shin pads, and padded compression shorts with athletic cups can protect you and make you more willing to be involved in the next river rescue. Shin pads and compression shorts are often worn under a dry suit, while elbow pads may be worn inside or outside the suit, depending on the design.

G-FORM

NORTHWEST
RIVER SUPPLIES

Splash Tops and Bottoms

Splash wear is essentially the same thing as a wind breaker or wind pants with the added element of being ready for a splash. During a swim, water flows through these garments with ease, making them non-waterproof for swimming. Splash wear is commonly worn over wet suits to help in colder environments.

NORTHWEST
RIVER SUPPLIES

Dry Suits, Dry Tops, and Dry Pants

Anyone responding to cold water river rescues should ideally be in a dry suit. Dry suits are safety gear, and will often make the difference when attempting an effective swim-based rescue. Sewn-in waterproof socks or latex booties mean feet can be warm and dry. Relief zippers are well worth the extra cost.

KOKATAT

LEVEL 6

Insulation
Advanced synthetic fabrics offer the ultimate thermal base layer. Different weights deliver varying levels of warmth without limiting your movements. Micro-fleece filaments efficiently wick moisture away from the skin, keeping you warm. Synthetic shirts, pants, union suits, and socks make excellent insulation underneath a dry suit.

NORTHWEST
RIVER SUPPLIES

Skull Caps

Even if you don't typically wear one of these while you are paddling on cold rivers, you should consider having one available for rescue needs. Having a good skull cap could greatly extend your in-water capabilities when it matters most.

NORTHWEST
RIVER SUPPLIES

Gloves and Hand Protection

Just like we put on medical gloves before handling a patient, we should also consider gloves before rescue. If your hands don't work, neither do you. Cold fingers and uncomfortable hands make rescues more challenging. Even warm weather river rescue responses require hand protection to prevent damage from fast-moving rope. Slipping and falling on rocks can also injure the hands. Some glove designs have armor built into them to protect knuckles from damage.

NORTHWEST
RIVER SUPPLIES

Type I	TYPE I: OFF-SHORE
22 lb. flotation	Best for all waters. Good for open ocean, rough seas, or remote water, where rescue may be slow coming. Will keep unconscious person's head above water.

Type II	TYPE II: NEAR-SHORE
15.5 lb. flotation	For general boating activities. Good for calm, inland waters, or where there is a good chance for fast rescue.

Type III	TYPE III: FLOTATION AIDS
15.5 lb. flotation	For general boating or the specialized activity that is marked on the label (water skiing, fishing, canoeing, kayaking, etc.). Not all Type III PFDs work for all applications. Good for river running where the swimmer is capable of self-rescue and swimming herself to shore.

Type IV	TYPE IV: THROWABLE DEVICE
16-22 lb. flotation	These are often found in the form of a ring buoy or boat seat cushion. Some river sections will allow presence of a throw rope to meet any Type IV requirements.

Type V	TYPE V: SPECIAL USE DEVICE
15-25 lb. flotation	For river purposes, Type V usually means either additional flotation, or a harness releasable under load, or both. The two most common Type V categories are Rescue and Commercial. A rescue model is essentially a Type III with a releasable chest harness integrated into it. Commercial Type Vs have upwards of 25 lb. of flotation and a flotation flap/collar that helps keep the head above water when floating on one's back. These are commonly worn by customers of commercial rafting operations who have little to no experience swimming in whitewater.

As of 2014, the US Coast Guard has removed the type coding requirement for PFDs as a way to reduce confusion in the international marketplace. New labels have yet to be approved, however, and manufacturers will continue to use Type I–V coding until newer standards and labels are designed and approved.

PERSONAL FLOTATION DEVICES

While participating in boating activities, all participants should wear PFDs. PFDs should be sized and fitted for each individual before leaving for the water, and when worn, they need to be secured properly—all zippers, buckles, and ties fastened correctly. If fitted properly, the shoulders of the PFD should not come above the wearer's ears when pulled upward. In order for a PFD to work properly, it must be cared for properly; avoid sitting or standing on your flotation vest. Using PFDs as seats compresses the closed cell foam and abrades the fabric more quickly. Store all PFDs in a clean, dry place.

Consider referring to this gear as a personal flotation device or a PFD rather than a "life jacket." The device by itself will not save your life. We still need to have sound decision-making and judgment when operating in a river. Remember, the language we choose will shape and influence the thinking of our risk management culture.

PFD Classifications

The United States Coast Guard has five classifications for PFDs. They recommend different types for different applications. Make sure you are aware of the requirements for your area. Most adults need an extra 12 pounds of buoyancy to keep their heads above flat moving water. A PFD with 22 pounds of flotation can be thought of as a device that lifts up on the wearer with approximately 22 pounds of force.

Type V Rescue PFD

Type V rescue PFDs are essentially Type III PFDs with an integrated releasable chest harness that allows the rescuer to secure a rope to his torso but release quickly from it when needed.

Type V rescue PFDs were designed after several rescue fatalities that occurred in the 1980s and '90s where would-be rescuers drowned after the rope that was tied around their waists or hands got stuck on a midstream obstruction. Not being able to get free from the rope created a fatal entrapment scenario. Tying a rope around someone, or even wrapping it around the hand, prior to getting into moving current is a fatal mistake. This should be well known by everyone participating in any river activity. Prevention is key.

Type V rescue PFDs are essential tools for experienced whitewater paddlers and those working in the river rescue industry. However, like specialized gear used in other sports, the safety features of a Type V rescue PFD require training and experience to be useful; without the necessary skills, they provide a false sense of security at best.

Most commercial river guiding operations outfit clients with Type III PFDs, because in the guiding context, there is not time to train clients on the use of Type Vs. Guides assume responsibility for their clients' well-being. However, just as familiarity with shovel, probe, and beacon are necessary for backcountry skiers, training and practice in the use of Type V rescue PFDs is essential for all those who make a habit of frequenting whitewater.

See Part Two for more information on how to use these PFDs.

Key features to look for in a Type V rescue PFD include:

- Harness: It should have a well-reviewed, integrated release system.
- Knife patch: PFDs come with knife patches for securing river-specific knives to them. Consider the location of the knife patch as it relates to your preferences.
- Adjustability: Clothing layers change throughout the year. Choose a PFD that allows you to easily adjust to accommodate varying clothing thickness.
- Gear pockets: Look for storage for knives, carabiners, and webbing.

ASTRAL
BUOYANCY

EXTRASPORT

RESCUE KNIVES AND SAWS

Knives

Rescuers should regularly ask themselves, "Am I ready to deal with an entrapment?" You can answer this question by considering both practiced skills and available equipment. Gear and ropes regularly cause entrapments on rivers. Having a readily-available knife is a critical responsibility of all river runners and rescuers. Carrying a throw bag without a knife is reckless. If you may possibly throw a rope to a patient in the river, you need to be prepared for it to get hung up on rocks, trees, and man-made objects beneath the surface.

Your primary knife should be readily available to both hands and releasable to either hand. It's usually located directly on the outside of the PFD or on a separate belt to allow for easy access if you should need to cut yourself free. (Many riverbeds have rope stuck in them from years of use, and now free rope ends float undetected below the surface, ready to grab on to unsuspecting swimmers.) You should also carry a collapsible backup knife.

Many styles are available. Features to consider include:

- **Pointed or blunt tip.** Pointed tips allow for quicker puncture cuts when working on inflatables but pose considerable threat of injury to everyone on scene. Blunt tips reduce this hazard and allow rescuers to be slightly more aggressive when cutting rope.
- **One edge or two.** Some rescuers like both edges sharp and ready to go. Others prefer to reduce risk of injury by having only one cutting edge.
- **Serrated or smooth edge.** Some rescuers prefer the serrated edge for cutting, but serrated edges cannot be sharpened when dull. Others recognize a straight edge cuts just as effectively and is easy to sharpen.

NORTHWEST
RIVER SUPPLIES

COLUMBIA
RIVER KNIFE
& TOOL

- **Ease of release.** A variety of sheaths exist, each with its own unique securing mechanism for releasing the knife. Play with the release and determine which is most comfortable and operable for you.

Some will argue that your rescue knife should only be used for rescue purposes. But how do you know if your knife is sharp unless you cut an apple with it? How natural will it be to release it in a true emergency if you don't make a regular habit of reaching for it to know where it is and how it releases? Consider using your knife regularly for all purposes while constantly evaluating its cutting power.

SAWS

Strainers are a hazard on all rivers. Each rescuer should have ready access to a saw in the event of a patient getting stuck on a strainer. Ideally, this would be the rescuer's own saw that she's practiced cutting with before. It should be stored in an obvious and accessible location; when seconds count, you want to be able to relieve the strainer or cut the branches causing the entrapment. Saws are also effective for cutting the tube of a raft or the end of a plastic kayak. Simple saw types for consideration include:

   Folding camp saw. Offers quick set-ups and classic pull-and-push cutting technique.

   Pocket chainsaw. These slick cutters offer a collapsible construction and require little storage space. They deploy quickly and cut aggressively.

GERBER
GEAR

UST
BRANDS

WHISTLE

PFDs are often sold with a free emergency whistle. Blowing on these offerings can sometimes sound like a toy train in a kindergarten class. This is a critical piece of gear and intentional thought should be put into its design, placement, and attachment. Fox 40 offers a brilliant design, featuring a powerful blast heard easily over whitewater. There are no moving parts in it that can freeze together, swell with water, or disintegrate over time. It will also self-clear if it fills with water. These whistles are very affordable and used worldwide by rescue agencies. A simple flex coil attachment with low breaking strength helps prevent the whistle from causing an entrapment if it's worn while swimming through a rapid.

These plastic recoiling lanyards do a nice job of keeping a whistle available but also out of the way. FOX 40 INTERNATIONAL

RESCUE BELT

One-inch tubular webbing can be incredibly helpful in a variety of rescue scenarios as explained throughout this book. Each rescuer on scene should carry her own supply of webbing. It can be folded up and stored in a pocket, or it can be worn as a rescue belt.

Use a 15-foot piece of 1-inch tubular webbing and a locking carabiner to make your belt. Tie the webbing into a continuous loop using a water knot or overhand on a bend. Wrap the loop twice around your waist. Clip it using a locking carabiner, and be sure to check that it is locked on a regular basis. Non-locking carabiners present considerable entrapment concerns and should not be worn in an exposed location. Non-lockers should live in pockets when not in use.

PULLEYS

Each boat should carry a set of three high quality rescue pulleys, the minimum number required to build an acceptable 3:1 mechanical advantage. This is further explained in the Mechanical Advantage section of this book on page 220. Fully-loaded expedition rafts should consider a rack of five pulleys so that more advanced systems can be built to manage heavier boats.

1" Pulley

These lightweight options fit easily into cargo pockets yet are still incredibly strong. Designs with prusik-minding capability add significant functionality to mechanical advantage systems.

Material: high-quality aluminum
Strength: 22 kN = 4,946 lb.
Maximum rope diameter: 13 mm – 0.5"
Sheave: 1.2" plastic
Axle: solid stainless steel

2" Pulley

Big pulleys are stronger and create less friction than smaller pulleys. Sidewalls featuring a series of holes help to minimize hydroplaning that might otherwise occur with a typical pulley. Sealed ball bearings provide optimal efficiency.

Material: high-quality aluminum
Strength: 34 kN = 7,644 lb.
Maximum rope diameter: 13 mm – 0.5"
Sheave: 2" aluminum
Axle: ball bearing

Rigging Plate

Rigging plates can make building rope systems quicker and more organized. Connections can be made in all points and loaded in all directions. This is not essential gear but can be helpful. Some find teaching mechanical advantage systems to be an easier task when they use rigging plates.

Material: anodized aluminum
Strength: 52 kN = 11,700 lb.
Features: NFPA "G"—general use requirement of 36 kN

CARABINERS

Steel versus Aluminum Carabiners

Steel carabiners provide exceptional strength over aluminum versions, but they are also considerably heavier and more expensive. High-angle rope and rock rescue occur in the vertical realm and often mean rescuing people from considerable heights. Redundancy and extreme strengths make sense in this environment, since life is on the line. Swiftwater rescue operations requiring ropes and pulleys occur in the low-to-no angle environment and often set up with the goal of recovering boats from rocks, not people from heights. Aluminum meets most needs in river rescue.

Risks Involved with Non-Locking Carabiners

Non-locking carabiners have caused numerous injuries and near-misses. The temptation is to clip these tools onto PFDs and boats, so they are readily available when needed. The problem arises when you are accidently thrown into an object and unexpectedly clipped to some-thing you don't want to be attached to. This can happen while swimming through whitewater, for example, and the non-locking carabiner on your PFD hits an underwater shopping cart and pulls you to the bottom like an anchor. Non-locking carabiners should be stored in pockets and only employed for very intentional reasons when chances of entrapment are minimal. Even inside a boat, non-locking carabiners should be identified as potential entrapment hazards and possibly removed or swapped out for locking carabiners.

BLACK
DIAMOND

HOW GEAR STRENGTH IS RATED

The strength rating is the maximum force that a piece of gear can hold under perfect circumstances (ideal placement and correct loading). A Newton (N) is a measure of force, which equals mass times acceleration. A kilonewton (kN) equals 1,000 Newtons and is the typical unit of measurement found on rescue gear.

1 kN = approximately 225 lb. of force
16 kN = approximately 3600 lb. of force ∎

Type	Use	Strength
Oval 	All-around use, inexpensive.	Approx. 18 kN 4,050 lb.
Bent Gate 	Designed for easier clipping of a rope.	Approx. 24 kN 5,400 lb.
D-Shape 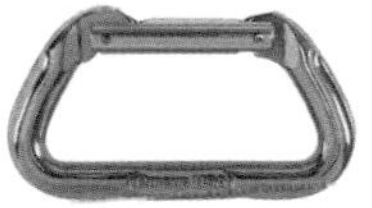	Lighter and stronger than ovals. Designed to hold the load off-center towards the strong spine. Make less functional pulleys than ovals when building certain types of systems.	Approx. 24 kN 5,400 lb.
Wire Gate 	Extremely lightweight. Snow and ice do not impair gate function. Wire gate prevents gate swing or gate whiplash.	Approx. 25 kN 5,625 lb.
Aluminum Screw Gate Locker 	The gate is locked closed by a manual locking mechanism that screws shut. These can be over-tightened and be difficult to unlock after being under load. These should be twist-locked only until resistance is first met to avoid over-tightening. They require double-checking on a regular basis to ensure they are locked.	Approx. 28 kN 6,300 lb.

OMEGA PACIFIC

(continued)

Type	Use	Strength
Steel Screw Gate Locker	Large D-shape creates a big gate opening, allowing it to handle gear easily. Incredible strength even with the gate open. These are common in professional response teams. Good for heavy duty haul systems on large boats or extrication systems. Very heavy and much more expensive than aluminum. These are often more than is necessary for most fast response river rescue operations. They exceed NFPA 1983, ANSI/OSHA strength requirements.	Approx. 72 kN 16,200 lb. closed 4,950 lb. open
Auto-Lockers	Come in a variety of styles and mechanisms. While some auto-lockers perform well in a mountain or rock environment, they struggle once exposed to water and sand. The spring loaded mechanisms will cease to operate rendering the locking mechanism useless. New technology continues to develop this option, as magnetic versions have shown promise. This style of carabiner still requires regular checks to ensure they are locked.	Full range of strengths

OMEGA PACIFIC

ROPE AND WEBBING

Modern rescue ropes are made from synthetic fibers like polypropylene, nylon, and polyester. The superiority of these synthetic materials over natural fibers has transformed rescue techniques. The construction style for most present-day rescue ropes is called kernmantle. The core (or kern) is a twisted parallel of fibers captured by a braided sheath (the mantle) that surrounds and protects it.

Choosing the type of rope depends on your application for it. Balancing the design features with construction type requires consideration of the following concepts:

- Flotation
- Strength
- Handling
- Visibility
- Durability

Ultra High Molecular Polyethylene (UHMP) fiber offers a relatively low-stretch rope with extremely high tensile strength. Common trade names for this kind of fiber include Dyneema and Spectra. While this kind of rope is almost three times as strong as polypropylene and floats just as well, it is very slippery and doesn't hold a knot well. So the sheaths of these ropes are made of the more knot-friendly polypropylene.

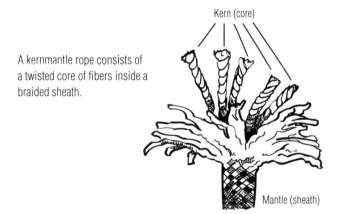

Kern (core)

A kernmantle rope consists of a twisted core of fibers inside a braided sheath.

Mantle (sheath)

Rope Strength, Knots, and Strength Loss

Rope fibers are oriented with the vertical axis of the rope for maximum strength. When these fibers are pulled on their horizontal axis, a significant amount of strength is lost. This is why knots reduce the overall tensile strength of a piece of rope and why we choose certain knots for specific applications. When a rope bends over a pulley or carabiner, strength reduction occurs. Generally speaking, the knots covered in this book reduce a rope's strength by approximately 30 percent.

Care and Storage of Rope

Inspect your ropes on a regular basis. Slide the entire rope through your hands, feeling for the integrity of the core inch by inch. Visually inspect the

HAUL LINES FOR MECHANICAL ADVANTAGE SYSTEMS

¼" (6 mm) Dyneema 	Polypropylene sheath adds buoyancy and protects the high-strength Dyneema core. **Tensile strength:** 2,495 lb. **Elongation:** dynamic or 1.4% at 300 lb.
⅜" (9 mm) Dyneema 	Polypropylene sheath adds buoyancy and protects the high-strength Dyneema core. **Tensile strength:** 5,239 lb. **Elongation:** dynamic or 1.4% at 300 lb.
½" (12 mm) Polyester	High performance, durability, low elongation, and suppleness. Bigger and heavier option to carry. Do you need a rope that breaks at 9,000 lb. if your system has aluminum carabiners that break at 4,050 lb.? **Tensile Strength:** 9084 lb. **Elongation:** none (static) **Features:** certified to NFPA 1983, 2006 48-carrier sheath construction

STERLING ROPE

sheath as you go, looking for damage or excessive abrasions. The decision to retire a rope is a subjective one, remembering that what is acceptable in a river rescue or for pulling a boat stuck on a rock may be different than what is acceptable in other pursuits, like rock climbing. Keep your ropes clean. The dirtier the river, the more often you'll have to clean your ropes. Ropes should be rinsed with clean water after each trip. Allow them to air dry in a shady place before putting them away. Store ropes in a cool, dry place that is free of chemicals and out of direct sunlight. No matter how well you care for your ropes, they will eventually need to be retired. Retiring climbing ropes that protect people from falling is different than retiring a throw bag that swings swimmers into shore. Read the manufacturer's recommendations, and use your judgment, as well.

Prusik Cord
Prusik cords are used in mechanical advantage systems and are often pre-cut into a length between 36 and 48 inches. The diameter of this cord should be two-thirds the diameter of your haul line; for a 9-millimeter haul

line, use a 6-millimeter prusik. A 3:1 mechanical advantage system would require at least two of these prusiks. Store prusik cords, unknotted, in a small dry bag. Pre-tying these loops only stresses the rope longer and makes it fail more easily. The prusik is likely to be the weakest link in your system and the first thing to break if the system does fail. It should only take you another 20 to 30 seconds to tie a figure 8 on a bend for your prusik loop. Having them pre-tied doesn't save a lot of time, but it does accelerate the aging process of the rope and weakens it more quickly.

	6 mm 1,978 lb.
	7 mm 2,788 lb.
	8 mm 3,934 lb

STERLING ROPE

Nylon Tubular Webbing

Webbing is strong, tough, and inexpensive compared to rope. It is an excellent multi-purpose tool. Store it in a dry, clean place without any tight knots in it. Five 15-foot pieces are a good addition to a river rescue kit. Use a daisy chain hitch to store the webbing in a more manageable length, and then clip the five pieces together with one large carabiner. Some folks like to have different colors for different lengths: 5-foot lengths are green, 12-foot lengths are yellow, 15-foot lengths are blue, 20-foot lengths are red, and 25-foot lengths are black.

½"	1,000 lb. tensile strength (18 kN)
1"	4,300 lb. tensile strength (18 kN)
2"	7,100 lb. minimum tensile strength (32kN)

STERLING ROPE

These various lengths can be helpful in high-angle rope rescue where different precut lengths get applied to the same litters and same anchor systems routinely. In the river rescue arena, typically a simple rack of five 15-foot pieces will get the job done.

THROW BAGS

A throw bag is a small bag with a rope stuffed in it, often tossed to unintentional swimmers and used to pull them back to the boat or to shore. Throw bags are an essential piece of boating gear. They come in lengths of 30 to 80 feet (10 to 25 meters) and widths of ¼ to ⅜ inch. Strengths vary from 1,000 to 5,000 pounds (500 to 2,500 kilograms). Ropes can be made of nylon, polyester, polypropylene, or Dyneema. Different styles offer different advantages and trade-offs. Having a variety available on a rescue scene can open up options for strategies; it can also create confusion if everyone on scene isn't aware of appropriate uses for different types of cord. Each rescuer should have a high-quality throw bag. Features to consider include:

NORTHWEST RIVER SUPPLIES

- **Strength.** Each rescuer should carry her own haul line quality rope (more than 2,500 lb. tensile strength) to be used in potential extrications and mechanical advantage systems.
- **Girth.** Consider minimum ⅜-inch (9-millimeter) rope for ease of gripping with wet hands compared to ¼-inch rope.
- **Entrapment potential.** Eliminate and minimize loops on your throw bag's design to minimize the risk of snagging hands or underwater obstacles.

Description	Pros and Cons
70' of ¼" Poly 950 lb. NORTHWEST RIVER SUPPLIES	**Pros:** inexpensive, fast, and accurate to throw **Cons:** harder to hold onto under load and low breaking strength
70' of ¼" Dyneema 2608 lb. NORTHWEST RIVER SUPPLIES	**Pros:** fast, accurate, relatively high breaking strength **Cons:** harder to hold onto under load and more expensive
55' of ¼" Waist belt 950–2608 lb. NORTHWEST RIVER SUPPLIES	**Pros:** fast, accurate, secures to waist, comes in different strengths **Cons:** harder to hold and to stuff little bag, less usable rope
75' of ⅜" Polypropylene 1900 lb. NORTHWEST RIVER SUPPLIES	**Pros:** less expensive, easier to hold **Cons:** lower breaking strength, heavier to throw
75' of ⅜" Dyneema 5200 lb. NORTHWEST RIVER SUPPLIES	**Pros:** strong, easier to hold **Cons:** more expensive, heavier to throw
75' of ⅜" Liquid Logic Speedloader 1900 lb. LIQUID LOGIC	**Pros:** innovative, lightweight, compact, super fast re-loading of bag **Cons:** more expensive, low tensile strength

Specialized Equipment

ROPE RETRIEVAL SYSTEMS

In some rare, yet challenging, situations, accessing a rope that is fixed and floating in the current can dramatically improve possible solutions. Sometimes the rope can be hooked with a stick from shore, but when it's beyond the reach of rescuers, additional tools may be required.

A snag plate can be attached to your throw bag ropes and tossed out over the rope you are trying to retrieve. It snags the rope, and you haul it in.

WILD WATER SUPPLY

ROPE LAUNCHERS

Several options exist for getting a rope across a long distance. Some rope launchers can deploy a rope 300 to 500 feet, and then release an inflatable rescue ring after a water-sensitive carbon dioxide charge contacts the river. Other options include slingshots, bow and arrow accessories, and shot gun accessories.

The ResQmax Line Thrower can reach distances of 300 feet with a 6-millimeter polypropylene rope.
RESCUE SOLUTIONS INTERNATIONAL

SUPERCLIP RESCUE TOOL

The Superclip rescue tool is great for attaching a rope to a patient or piece of gear that is just out of reach. Secure the Superclip to a pole or paddle and position a locking carabiner into place with the gate open. Extend out and hook on to what you are trying to retrieve and simply pull back. Now the carabiner and rope are attached to the object you're trying to retrieve.

RIVER BOARD AND FINS

River boards designed specifically for river rescue offer a sturdy platform for two people and the integrity to withstand significant abuse in powerful hydraulics and sharp rocks. "Boogie boards" used at beaches for body surfing are generally much smaller in size and do not serve well as a rescue or stabilizing platform. It's common for rescue teams to become too dependant on river boards and fins when they really would be better off just swimming board-free. It's easier to make challenging moves and crawl around on rocks and surfaces without fins on your feet or a river board under your arm. River board application often make the most sense when needing to cover an extended distance of river while searching for patients.

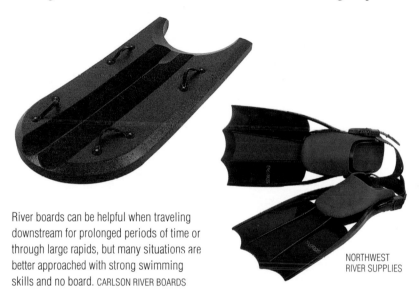

River boards can be helpful when traveling downstream for prolonged periods of time or through large rapids, but many situations are better approached with strong swimming skills and no board. CARLSON RIVER BOARDS

NORTHWEST RIVER SUPPLIES

HEADLAMPS AND FLASHLIGHTS

A fully waterproof headlamp is a useful piece of equipment, even when there is no plan to be on the river at night. Advancements in technology have generated a variety of lightweight, compact options that put out powerful spotlights that reach upwards of 200 to 300 feet out. You get what you pay for. Simple, inexpensive models have their place as a backup unit, but they are not rescue-worthy. Whether it's hiking out on a trail on a dark night or conducting night rescue operations in the river, you'll be thankful if you made the decision to

BLACK DIAMOND

spend the extra money to support your invaluable sense of vision. Consider a model that has spot, proximity, strobe, red light, and dimming settings. Remember a set of fresh backup batteries, and remind your team, too.

FIRST AID KITS

Rescue isn't just getting the person back to shore safely; it's also treating injuries effectively. Having a quality first aid kit is critical. River trips should consider having one for each boat. There is no perfect first aid kit available on the market today. Each trip to the river requires unique considerations based on the environment, location, and duration of the trip. The number of people on the trip, their ages, experience, training, medical histories, and medications are also important considerations.

Other first aid kit considerations:

- Lightweight shelter or bivy sack
- Multi-use or hard-to-improvise items, like tape and trauma shears
- Drybag or plastic water bottle to store first aid kit in and keep it dry
- Light sticks
- Plastic zip ties for fixing gear, improvising solutions, building splints
- Parachute cord (bright orange, yellow, or red) for flagging trails, clothesline, splints, shelter, gear repair etc.
- Duct tape
- Fire starter (e.g., cotton balls soaked in Vaseline)
- Compass
- Signal mirror
- Extra layers, gloves, balaclava
- Water treatment (e.g., chlorine bleach, iodine tablets, portable filter, etc.)
- Portable stove (e.g., Jetboil) and freeze-dried meals (e.g., Mountain House)
- Food (e.g., sugar, snacks, coffee singles, etc.)

ADVENTURE
MEDICAL KITS

Entrapment Alert:
Mitigate the Risk of Gear Causing Harm

Whenever you purchase new equipment, be sure to enjoy the moment as you take it out of its packaging and envision the disappearance of your last paycheck. Soon afterwards ask yourself the question, "What's wrong with my new gear?" It doesn't matter if it's the latest and greatest version, there usually will be something that could use improvement. When manufacturers are designing the next year's model of any particular piece of gear, one of the easiest ways to make it stand out from previous versions is to simply add extra zippers, bells, whistles, and sometimes generally unnecessary bling. Examine your gear closely, and look for some of the following hazards:

Unnecessary loops. Consider minimizing unnecessary fixed loops on your gear and in your boat. Loops invite entrapment. And they appear to be everywhere. They are on helmets, PFDs, soft gear, hard gear, and on our boats. Minimize loops, and you will minimize entrapment potential.

Loose perimeter lines. The perimeter line on your raft should be tied such that it is tight like a guitar string. Loose perimeter lines invite entrapment. (Note: The perimeter line should not be referred to as a "chicken line," as some call it, since it doesn't support a culture of risk management to shame someone for holding onto the boat.)

Non-locking carabiners. Exposed non-locking carabiners also pose a real threat to everyone in a river environment. When placed carelessly, they can present considerable entrapment potential and can clip into sandals, boats, D-rings, shopping carts, cyclone fencing, rebar, and numerous other things that we'd rather not be attached to. Even carabiners attaching water bottles to rafts should ideally be locking carabiners, since kicking these with your shoes can accidently result in getting clipped into the raft as it is flipping upside-down. A common mistake is to place non-locking carabiners on the lapels of PFDs (including the non-locking carabiners sold on kayak tow tethers) where they are readily available to clip into anything else in this world. The strong case for non-locking carabiners is that it is easy to clip them in and out of things. This is also precisely the argument against them. The three to four seconds it takes to unlock the carabiner before use should not be a deal breaker in your rescue scenario. Keep in mind too that just because you have a locking carabiner doesn't mean you always have to lock it. But having the ability to do so when it can only improve the risk management in your scenario is extremely valuable.

■ A RIVER NARRATIVE: THE CHEOAH RIVER

By Charlie Walbridge

The Cheoah River in western North Carolina is a serious Class IV run: bigger, faster, and more relentless than most of the rivers and creeks in the region. Thanks to the efforts of American Whitewater, there are regular water releases from the dam that controls river flow. I'd been making my way down the river and getting pushed around a lot when I eddied out above a long, boulder rapid leading into 15-foot-high Bear Creek Falls. Concerned that I might flip, miss my roll, and wash over this gnarly drop, I took out and started to carry. As I walked, I watched a young man flip, bail out, and swim. He managed to clamber out on a small rock right at the lip of the falls!

The rock was about the size of the roof of a Volkswagen Bug, so the stranded paddler was safe for now. But the water was scheduled to run for another 36 hours! A crowd gathered. Someone went downriver to fetch the Nantahala Outdoor Center's Cheoah Raft guides, and while we waited, I tried to figure out what to do. Helping this guy out was going to be challenging. The river was almost 500 feet wide, so setting up a Telfer lower would require over 600 feet of half-inch static rescue line and lots of hardware. That's not stuff that even NOC was likely to have around.

Swimmer rescued on The Cheoah River, North Carolina. CHARLIE WALBRIDGE

An hour later the NOC guides finally arrived. Led by Trip Leader Shane Williams, they ferried across the river, rigged an anchor on a large tree, and began lowering their raft towards the trapped paddler. I'd mentally rejected the idea of a straight lower to the lip of the falls because there was no place directly upstream to anchor the raft, but Shane and his crew had a different plan. As the lower proceeded, two paddlers inside the raft used draw strokes to pull the boat out into the current. It swung out, pendulumed back into the eddy, then with the help of those draw strokes swung out again. With each swing the raft was lowered a bit more until it hung just above the trapped paddler. The man leaped to safety and the raft swung back to shore. What a slick rescue from a tough spot with minimal gear!

Charlie Walbridge began running rivers in the early 1960s and has made significant contributions to both river rescue curriculum and equipment design. He is the former safety chairman of the American Canoe Association and currently serves on the board of directors for the American Whitewater Affiliation. ■

CHAPTER 6

THE ANATOMY OF A RIVER

Hydraulics and Hazards 101

When traveling in, on, and around rivers, it is important to have a firm understanding of hydrology, a river's anatomy, and advanced concepts involved with our relationship to the currents. This chapter helps define typical river hazards and describes some techniques you must master to successfully mitigate these hazards. Having a clear and conceptual understanding of river anatomy and hydrology is the foundation of successful river rescue operations.

The West Branch of the Penobscot River, Maine.

CURRENT

Current is the flow of water in a river. The flow is the volume of water measured at a specific spot in cubic feet per second (cfs) or cubic meters per second (cms).

VELOCITY

The speed of the current measured in distance per time such as miles per hour (mph) or kilometers per hour (kph) is the velocity. The terrain influences velocity. A steeper gradient equals a faster current—use topographic maps to anticipate areas of steeper gradient. Wide sections of rivers decrease the velocity of the current, whereas narrow sections may increase it. Current tends to slow in deeper areas of a river.

When the speed of the river doubles, the force of the water is quadrupled against our bodies, and wading becomes exponentially more hazardous. One assessment tool for estimating current speed is to throw a stick into the main current and walk next to it on the bank. If the stick goes faster than walking pace, the current is likely too strong to wade. If the stick matches walking pace, the current might be slow enough to wade.

VOLUME

Volume is determined by the size of the watershed and seasonal factors like spring melt or periods of heavy rain. A high volume of water has much greater force than low volume of water in the same river.

DEPTH

The depth of a river is determined by gradient, riverbed configuration, and volume. Steeper gradients typically mean shallower depth, but faster current, whereas flatter gradients indicate greater depth and slower current. Unstable riverbeds may have deeper channels scoured out by the current; these channels may not be obvious from shore and may not be seen while crossing until you step into them.

A narrow river channel can constrict the volume of water to create greater depth. Conversely, a wide river channel can allow the volume of the river to spread out and create shallower depth.

RIVERBANKS

Banks that are steep or tall may indicate a deeper channel while riverbanks that are undercut may point to a strong current. The riverbank can present significant obstacles for people entering or exiting a river during a crossing or responding to a mishap.

FLUCTUATIONS

The volume of a river can change drastically over the course of a day, a season, or a year. Spring (and early summer in the mountains) is generally when the water can be at its highest and fastest. During late summer and fall seasons, after most of the winter snow has melted, river levels are usually lower and the current is slower.

Diurnal (happening during the day) fluctuations in river flow can occur due to changes in temperature and corresponding snowmelt rates. They are most pronounced during spring and early summer in locations with broad daily temperature fluctuations, such as mountain streams at high altitude and mid-latitude. Typically, a river rises as the heat of the day melts snow, which increases runoff. In the morning hours, following cooler nighttime temperatures, the river level is lower. Rivers at high latitude generally have smaller diurnal fluctuations because the long summer days have much smaller daily temperature fluctuations. Diurnal flow patterns can be gauged by placing a marker such as a stick or rock cairn at the water level and checking it periodically over a twelve to forty-eight hour period to see when the water level rises or falls.

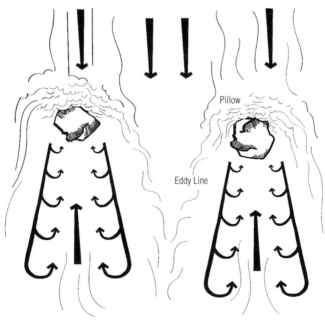

Anatomy of an eddy.

Constrictions can create strong downstream Vs like the one seen here.

EDDIES

This river feature is one that rescuers will find helpful when it comes to negotiating rapids. Eddies are formed on the downstream side of solid objects, such as rocks or part of the riverbank that is deflecting out into the current. An eddy is the relatively calm pocket of water found just below these obstructions. The obstruction creates a barrier in the current, deflecting water around it; gravity and diffusion cause slow-moving water to fill back in behind the barrier. The differential between the two currents is called the eddy line. The speed of the eddy water as it travels back upstream can vary considerably. Calmer eddies are often used to minimize the distance of a river crossing when wading across a river, or to stop downstream progress when paddling or swimming ("eddying out"). As we become better rescuers, we become more adept at catching eddies to make rapids more manageable. Midstream eddies essentially divide a large river into smaller, more manageable channels.

GLASSY VERSUS CRASHING WAVES

Glassy waves are smooth top to bottom, whereas crashing waves can have a constant aerated pile on top or progress from glassy to crashing. ∎

A series of tall standing waves are often created by one significant rock or ledge system upstream. The obstruction creates the first big wave, and the waves below it get smaller and smaller as the reactions dissipate. Tall waves that move or disappear from time to time may be simply reactionary waves caused by pressure.

WAVES

Generally speaking, waves are the result of increased water flow over some type of obstruction. They are vary in their size, shape, and behavior. They can be smooth or breaking, flat or steep, stationary or dynamic, predictable or ever-changing. All waves have a trough, face, and peak or crest.

In the case of standing waves, one obstruction in the riverbed will create the first big wave, and a train of subsequent waves will follow behind.

HOLES

Holes (also referred to as hydraulics, reversals, stoppers, pourovers, keepers, and low-head dams) are created when water goes over a submerged object, such as a rock or ledge. The water hits the river bottom on the downstream side of the object and cycles back upstream. This creates water that is now going the opposite direction of the main current.

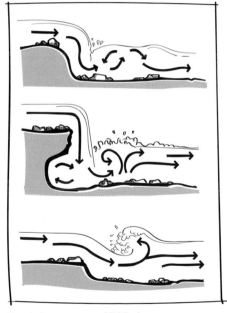

Top: A steep pourover. *Middle:* A pourover with subsequent upstream back carving of the bedrock; holes are sometimes more complicated than they appear. *Bottom:* A wave hole generally has an entrance that is less steep than a pourover but can still pack a powerful punch to a swimmer or boater.

How a hole looks on the surface offers clues to what's happening below.

Depending on how large the hole is, the resulting circular current can be quite strong and may be able to hold on to buoyant objects, such as a boat or a swimmer.

ROCKS ABOVE AND BELOW THE SURFACE

Large rocks that can be seen above the surface of the water are much easier to recognize than rocks under the surface. To help locate rocks beneath the surface, look for some type of disturbance or inconsistency on the surface of the water. When paddling, look downstream and pick a path on the river that avoids rocks. If hitting or coming up against a rock is unavoidable, aggressively lean the boat into the rock. This exposes the hull of the boat, instead of the deck, to the oncoming current. A boat in this position has less chance of wrapping around or pinning against the rock. Continue to lean the boat into the rock using body strength to hug the rock. Try to use your upper body to work your way around the rock while continually leaning your boat into the rock.

UNDERCUTS, LEDGES, AND SIEVES

Undercut rocks or ledges occur when water wears away at the rock or a bank, leaving a large portion sticking out above the waterline and a smaller, narrower portion below. Soft sedimentary rock tends to erode more quickly; therefore, it is quite common to find undercut rocks on rivers that flow through this type of rock. Undercut rocks and banks are usually found on the outside of bends.

The danger of undercuts is that a swimmer or a boat can be pushed into them and get stuck. The absence of a pillow on the upstream side of a rock can be an indicator of an undercut. (A pillow is water that builds up against a rock obstruction, climbing high onto it before falling back onto itself. Pillows will sometimes be foamy with aerated water.) With undercut rocks, there is little or no resistance to the oncoming water; it simply slips beneath the overhanging rock, so a pillow will not be formed. A sieve (a pile of rocks or debris with water flowing through it) is similar to a strainer or undercut in that it allows water to pass but solid objects become entrapped. Paddle or swim aggressively away from undercuts and sieves.

Over time, rivers wear away rocks below the surface and create significant hazards for anyone on a river. Undercut rocks will not have as large of an upstream pillow or an eddy on the downstream side as would be expected from their above-water size. These are potentially dangerous traps in the river; avoid them when possible.

Strainers

Strainers are one of the most lethal of river features. These dynamic and sometimes transient killers can occur on any river. Everyone on the river should be able to identify strainers and appreciate that even the seemingly benign versions can be death traps. Rescuers should understand what to do if one is encountered and how to respond to patients stuck in them.

A strainer is any object in a river that does not impede the flow of water but will catch, or strain, solid objects such as a boat or boater. The most common strainers are trees, shrubs, and tree roots. Rock piles can also create a strainer effect and have resulted in many fatalities. Man-made objects such as fences, fishing nets, shopping carts, vehicles, and old dam structures can also create deadly strainers. Rivers are naturally occurring conveyor belts with all types of objects falling into them regularly. Rescuers must be in constant anticipation of strainers, and rescue briefings should include this reminder.

Strive to avoid strainers, but train with your team and be ready for this worst-case scenario.

LOCATIONS OF STRAINERS

Strainers can occur anywhere on a river, but are most likely to be trees on the outside of bends. Since water speed increases on the outside of bends, it erodes or undercuts a bank, removing the dirt that supports trees. Once enough erosion has occurred, trees lean over or fall into the river. Trees can pile up on the outside of the bend, or they can break free and float to form a log jam downstream. In this exposed position, branches, trunks, and the exposed root system can all act as strainers. Because the roots are most likely to snag the bottom, trees tend to lie parallel to the current, with the roots facing upstream and the trunk downstream.

Headwaters or upper sections of rivers have great potential for strainers. The channels are often narrow and winding, with blind turns. Trees are easily caught and sometimes create river-wide strainers. Lower sections of large rivers that braid and meander can have logjams and strainers on undercut banks. Avoiding these can be less difficult because the river channel is usually wide, and the hazard is visible from some distance. Find out as much strainer information as possible prior to going to the river. Any new strainers identified should be publicized on paddler websites and posted at the put-in. It is important to remember that strainers and logjams can form in different locations from year to year.

STRAINER MANAGEMENT

The best tactic with strainers is to avoid them. If a strainer is identified downstream, try to stay clear of it by paddling or swimming away aggressively. Rescue scenes should have protection set near strainers should any rescuers or patients get swept toward them. Rescue saws capable of quickly cutting wood and plastic are a part of essential rescuer PPE.

STRAINER TYPES

There are two general types of strainers: *static* and *dynamic*.

Static strainers are fixed objects in the current. Trees that are still rooted to the riverbank but have fallen into the current, or fences, dock systems, and vehicles that are positioned in a fixed place in the river are examples of static strainers. Most static strainers eventually become dynamic strainers.

Dynamic strainers have been released into the current and travel silently downstream, posing incredible risk. These can be trees that have broken off after a long period as a static strainer, or trees and branches picked up during a flood stage. Dynamic strainers can be over one hundred feet long and have thirty-foot branches sticking up into the sky, or they can be waterlogged and cruise just below the surface. They also have the potential of quickly becoming static should they get trapped against the riverbank or a midstream obstruction.

Strainers are one of the greatest hazards on the river, due to high potential for entrapment and low visibility from an upstream perspective.

SELF-RESCUE

Prevention is key and strainers should be avoided at all costs. Things do happen, however, and if you find yourself coming upon a strainer quickly, you have a few options. Many organized river rescue classes practice these moves in a relatively safe, semi-controlled setting.

Option 1: Swim away aggressively. Don't look at the strainer, look at where you want to go, and swim like there is a crocodile chasing you. Don't flail. Use controlled aggressive crawl strokes and a constant flutter kick to keep moving efficiently across the surface of the water.

Option 2: Aggressively climb over it. If encountering the tree is inevitable, and it is a smaller diameter tree, you can attempt to swim at it and aggressively pull yourself over the top. Unless you *know* the underside is clear, avoid swimming under the tree. Approach the tree from upstream

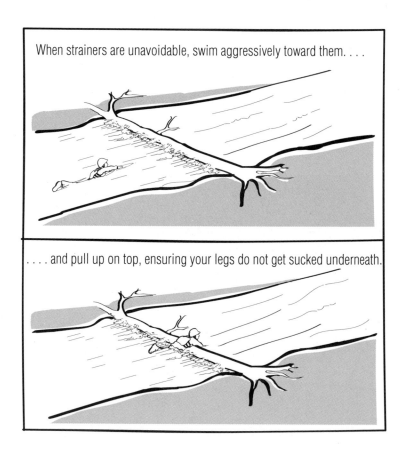

When strainers are unavoidable, swim aggressively toward them. . . .

. . . . and pull up on top, ensuring your legs do not get sucked underneath.

When practicing the stall and sidestep technique, try to find a slick, worn log to increase the realism. Practice in reasonable terrain and remember many things are often easier said than done.

by turning over on your stomach, with your head downstream, and swim aggressively at it while kicking hard to keep your feet on the upper surface. As you reach the tree, push down on it hard, and throw your hips up on the trunk, while continuing to kick. Rip, claw, and climb yourself over it, doing whatever it takes to stabilize your airway above the surface. (See illustration.) This is a very risky move that may not work.

Option 3: Stall and side step. If encountering the strainer is inevitable, and it is a larger diameter tree that is too big to climb over or it is clogged with too much debris, you can try the stall and sidestep. Swim as far to the exit side of the tree as you can before encountering it. Then, before contact, lie on your back perfectly flat with your feet downstream. It is critical that your body is totally flat or this will not work as well. Place your feet on the tree and allow yourself to stall out there, and then carefully and gently walk yourself to the exit side of the strainer.

STRAINERS: GROUP MANAGEMENT STRATEGIES FOR RIVER RUNNERS

We should be anticipating strainers on the outside of every turn we approach. This is where the banks receive the most damage resulting in trees falling into the water. Hug the inside corner until you can confirm the presence or absence of any strainers. Strainers kill boaters and tubers every year.

Training on a simulated strainer in a semi-controlled environment.

Boats should travel with enough space between them, so they can maneuver and avoid obstacles. On narrow, winding rivers, this might mean you will not be able see all the boats in your group or even the boat directly in front of or behind you. Approach blind turns with care and on the inside of the turn in case a strainer is just around the corner. When paddling river sections with known high strainer potential, consider organizing paddle teams to set up the strongest combinations possible and have the best boaters in the lead and sweep boats. If you have a strong team, place a talented rescuer in a boat in the middle of the group as well.

Practice relaying river signals with your team. The lead boat gives a paddle signal and the boat behind should respond. This should continue until the sweep boat has received the signal and responded. If the lead boat gives a stop signal, all of the following boats should stop as soon as possible in an appropriate place. If a directional signal is given boats should go in the direction indicated, left or right. As in any river setting, good trip awareness is vital.

Flood Stage and Big Water Concerns

When rivers flood, people get into trouble. Sometimes people wind up in the path of a flood accidentally, as when a bridge washes out as a motorist crosses over. Other times, it's planned trouble—a group of paddlers launching on a river during high spring run-offs. River rescuers need to preplan for big water events and appreciate that this is a specialized area of a dangerous discipline. Two of the biggest concerns that need to occupy the minds of rescuers during high water responses are *debris* and *helical flow*.

DEBRIS/STRAINERS AT FLOOD STAGE

The higher the water level, the higher the river is on the banks, and the more debris gets pulled into the current. This means a high volume of dynamic strainers traveling rapidly downstream that may be difficult to see because of large wave trains. Is the present water level on the rise or the decline? A rising level is generally more dangerous, as each successive inch of rise pulls more debris into the water. Once the flow begins to subside, the river is not as likely to collect more. For example, 50,000 cfs and rising is more dangerous than hitting the same 50,000 cfs two weeks later on the way back down from 80,000 cfs.

Flooding also results in all varieties of unnatural debris entering the river. This includes dock systems, trash cans, buoys, vehicles, trailers, fences, and livestock. At normal flows, the eddies created at the bottoms of rapids are often considered a place to set safety and where boats will intentionally eddy out while waiting for the rest of the boats to come through. However, at flood stage, an eddy can be overrun with large trees and debris, making it a hazardous place to be in or out of a boat.

Running rivers at flood stage could result in swimming in big water. Here rafters take on Lava Falls Rapid on the Colorado River deep inside the Grand Canyon. SACHA JACKSON

Forest fires can be an additional wildcard in assessing the likelihood of strainers in the river. A big wildfire the previous summer usually results in a much more dangerous spring run-off, as all contributing tributaries have been grossly compromised in stability. High levels of debris, soot, and sediment can be anticipated in any spring following a big fire season. Idaho saw an enormous fire in 2007, and it showed in the spring of 2008 with large amounts of dark, woody water.

Knives, trauma shears, and saws are always essential river gear. At flood stage they are especially important because of severe entrapment danger. Each rescuer should have a readily available collapsible saw to cut strainers and/or boat parts and a knife to deal with ropes. Professional response units should also consider having chain saws on hand for large strainers.

HELICAL FLOW AT FLOOD STAGE

The danger of helical flow is often wildly underestimated at flood stage and can be the ultimate killer on big water. In big water, many of the rapids will wash out, and wide open sneaks will become available along the sides of the rapids. However, at the same time, big flow rates mean that calm stretches between the rapids disappear. In addition, strong helical flows can drag swimmers under the surface while rebounding currents prevent them from getting to shore. Often the run-out below the rapids is more challenging than the rapids themselves. Huge eddy lines, tall eddy fences, six-foot-deep whirlpools, and debris collections within the eddy itself all contribute to compromising our ability to "set safety" below rapids as we normally do. We're often working much harder and with higher levels of stress just managing our boats in these eddies than we are going down the river.

Other objective hazards during big water include:

Current. The speed of water during flood stage can range from 10 mph to over 30 mph, depending on the volume, gradient, and constrictions. High current speeds often mean long swims and more danger of flush drowning. Flush drowning is a major killer in big water boating. The lead boat is the least protected. If people fall out of the lead boat, or it flips, who will collect them or get to them in time? It's worth discussing having a safety boater in a big kayak if you decide to run big water raft trips.

Hypothermia. Long swims mean an increased danger of hypothermia. Dry suits become important safety gear. We should be dressing for water temperature, not air temperature. We should be dressing for longer, colder swims and our ability to perform after we get out of the water. There is no comparison between the comfort of a swimmer in a dry suit versus a swimmer in a wet suit when it comes to cold, big water runoff. Although they are expensive, if you are trying to decide whether or not to launch on a big, cold water river trip, one of the considerations should be whether everyone has a dry suit. There are a number of places that these can be rented, and everyone on the trip should be prepared for an unintentional big water swim.

SUBJECTIVE HAZARDS OF BIG WATER

Once objective hazards have been addressed, it's equally important to consider the two most important subjective hazards in this equation: the team's experience on big water and the leader's experience on big water.

Big Water: Group Management Strategies for River Runners

- Modify safety talk to incorporate big water concerns and self-rescue techniques.
- Choose good locations to practice big water swimming. It's important to identify strong versus weak swimmers early on in the trip— for both group- and self-awareness.
- Spend extra time training crews how to stay in the boat. Drill on the "Get down!" command. All rafts should have a tightly threaded

The infamous Lava Falls on the Colorado River of the Grand Canyon at 21,000 cfs.
SACHA JACKSON

Scouting is a great opportunity to continue to grow as a team. Appreciate that you are not only scouting the rapid, but also scouting the present climate of your risk management culture.

- Make sure you know where you and others will be in the running order.
- Decide where you will regroup at the bottom of the rapid.

Once a rapid has been scouted and decisions made on routes and safety, decide how the group will actually run the rapid. There are several different approaches to running rapids; which one you use will depend on the rapid itself. Common approaches are one-at-a-time or follow-the-leader.

Running one boat at a time works well when stronger paddlers need to be placed in strategic points throughout the rapid for safety. The lead boat runs the rapid first. Throw bags may be placed at certain points in the rapid for safety set up. Run the rapid one at a time on paddle signals. Make sure everyone knows who will be running the rapid when. Always designate who will run the rapid last.

At some rapids running follow-the-leader style is appropriate. This means there are designated lead and sweep boats, and all other boats are spaced in between. This style works well on less technical rapids or a rapid that is long, thus making it difficult to use paddle signals. An abbreviated version of this works well with rafts and kayaks. The rafts run the rapid first and place safety at the bottom, and all the kayakers or one kayak pod run next.

Whichever method you decide upon at a rapid, make sure everyone is clear on the route, how safety will work, and what style you will use to run the rapid.

LEADERSHIP AND SCOUTING

Scouting and running rapids allows everyone to make choices and take personal responsibility for decisions they have made. The intent is to develop guidelines to use in future experiences, not hard and fast rules. This provides an excellent avenue to develop judgment and decision-making. Initiating discussions at rapids allows for teamwork and communication.

■ A RIVER NARRATIVE: HESS RIVER CANOE ADVENTURE

By Geoff Kooy

Traveling a big northern river by canoe is always an adventure. The whitewater tends to be on the easier end of the spectrum, but things can still go wrong quickly. With the combination of cold temperatures, fast current, and extreme remoteness, even a Class II rapid can give you pause. Leading a group of beginner canoeists into this environment adds to the recipe for excitement. Consistent communication between all group members is a must. Instructors need to demonstrate a high level of situational awareness and have multiple rescue scenario plans in place. When things go wrong, there is very little time to group up, formulate a plan, and proceed.

One summer we were running a NOLS canoe course on the Hess River in the Yukon Territory. This is a place that few people ever travel. The options for the put-in are either a very expensive flight or to drag your boats up a creek for four days to get to the headwaters. There is little available information or guidebooks for this run. Emergency evacuations require a helicopter. It's remote. It's beautiful. It's wild.

Early in the course, and still actively coaching and developing canoe skills, we came to a canyon section and decided to do some intensive training on front ferrying. My co-instructor Rebecca and I demonstrated the ferry skill first and then stayed together in the boat to act as safety while the students practiced. As anticipated, one of the boats flipped and two students swam for shore with their paddles. Rebecca and I chased the boat.

We clipped into the capsized canoe with our tow system and began hauling it for shore through a small recovery pool. Just below was a corner leading into an unknown canyon. Before getting securely into the eddy, the tow rope went taut, and the weight of the capsized canoe began to pull us downstream. Concerned about getting pulled out of the eddy—or worse, flipping our own boat—we released out of the tow system and watched the canoe quickly disappear around the corner.

We had a decision to make. Option A: Continue the retrieval attempt through an unknown canyon and further separate ourselves from the group. Option B: Abandon the canoe, regroup, and hope to find the canoe later downstream. Because we had established systems in place for just such an occurrence, we chose Option A. Our third instructor stayed with the student group while we pursued the boat.

Over the course of the next 10 kilometers, we tried repeatedly to tow the canoe to shore, and repeatedly we felt the tug of the capsized canoe before we were fully secure in an eddy. Several times, we encountered a situation where if we had not released the boat at the precise moment we did, we would have flipped our canoe for sure. We were navigating through Class II/III rapids, boat-scouting, trying to run the rapids efficiently and effectively, while chasing a canoe—all the while hoping it would not get stuck or pinned somewhere.

It took us a total of 11 kilometers before we finally got it towed all the way to shore. Needless to say, we were relieved to be finished and with all gear recovered. We positioned ourselves on a gravel bar and waited for the rest of the group to catch up to us. But as it turned out, this little adventure was just getting started.

The third instructor, Gary, and our fifteen students—all midshipmen from the US Naval Academy—proceeded downstream after watching our chase disappear around the corner. Two of the students were without a boat or their personal gear, and so the group lined around rapids and proceeded slowly and conservatively. Despite their risk management efforts, a boat got away from them at one of the bigger rapids and flipped. They decided not to chase it, since the terrain downstream was unknown, and they knew we were down there and could possibly rescue the boat if we saw it in time.

We were still waiting for the group to catch up when we suddenly saw the capsized canoe making its way downriver. Again, we faced a decision with two options. Option A: Get back in our canoe and try to retrieve the boat. Option B: let the canoe float past us.

We chose Option B. The variables in our current situation had drastically changed. Four students were now without a boat or personal gear. We did not want to further distance ourselves from the group. True to risk management priorities, we chose people over gear.

While we were figuring out our options with this new development, the rest of the group with Gary was still far upstream. When the second boat flipped, Gary decided to call an immediate stop and set up camp on a sand bar. It was far from an ideal campsite, but he concluded that the group needed to stop and recoup from the day's events. We were still waiting for the group to catch up to us. By 7:00 p.m. we realized that this would not be happening today. We made a camp, had a fitful sleep, and early the next morning decided to travel upstream, up the canyon, to attempt to rendezvous with the group.

After a few hours travel, we finally saw the group, all in high spirits. We devised a plan of action to get the group through the remaining section of the canyon (we were still missing one canoe at this point) and camped shortly afterwards. The next day, river karma repaid our caution; we found the missing canoe stuck on a shallow gravel bar. All of the gear inside was even dry!

I think about this event often in my life as a river instructor. I even tell the tale quite often. I find that it is a good reminder for me to avoid complacency. Because of this event, and the success of it, I force myself every time to communicate with my instructor team and develop situational plans and strategies. We do not wait for an event to occur and then formulate a plan. Rather, we formulate plans and adapt them to the specific situation. And we practice our skills and train rigorously and constantly.

Geoff Kooy is a senior instructor and program supervisor for NOLS. He is a river rescue technician certified by Wilderness Rescue International. He leads canoeing, rafting, and kayaking trips across the globe. ∎

NOLS Instructors training in both river rescue and first aid scenarios. MOE WHITSCHARD

CHAPTER 7

WILDERNESS MEDICINE AND REMOTE RESCUE TRAINING

In Chapter 3 we discussed the principles of river rescue and introduced the Search and Rescue acronym of LAST (Locate, Access, Stabilize, and Transport). This sequence describes the events necessary to find and successfully rescue a patient. The majority of this text focuses on accessing patients in swiftwater terrain. However, once you do reach and extricate your patients from the river (and sometimes while doing so), you must be prepared to stabilize their condition and address any injuries they may have sustained. River rescuers need to have adequate training in first aid and CPR treatment principles before considering themselves rescue ready.

River rescue training + first aid training = qualified.

There are a number of first aid training options out there. Consider your training goals and your expected river trips as you decide which works best for you. You get what you pay for with classes, and while some online options are good for rounding out existing knowledge bases, there is really no better way to get the skills you need than to find a hands-on, practical course with quality educators. The goal is not to "check" first aid credentials off the list of things to do. Rather, the goal should be to prepare yourself to confidently respond to life-threatening scenarios in a challenging environment.

The NOLS Wilderness Medicine Institute (WMI) teaches wilderness medicine through a unique combination of lectures, case studies, demonstrations and practical scenarios. The curriculum is constantly updated, accurate, relevant and practical. Courses are rigorous and intensive. WMI prepares students to make sound decisions in remote places when resources are scarce and no help is on the way.

Wilderness medicine courses stress responding in backcountry contexts where resources are limited and the patient may be hours or days from definitive care. Ideally, all group members have wilderness medicine training, in large part because such training drives home the reality of how difficult it is to treat patients in a remote context. Prevention is an essential leadership skill. A thorough survey of the prevention and treatment of injury and in illness in the backcountry is beyond the scope of this book.

Courses at WMI—and throughout the wilderness medicine industry—are differentiated by their length, with longer courses providing more in-depth training. Course length and titles are standardized across the industry. Find a quality training provider, take the appropriate course for your needs, and then practice your skills relentlessly until proficiency is gained.

With that in mind, the following chapter is designed to canvass the range of wilderness first aid training options out there, and to provide treatment reference points for readers that are graduates of such programs. It is not intended to provide instruction to those without prior training.

WILDERNESS MEDICINE COURSE TYPES

Wilderness First Aid (WFA). Sixteen hours of basic first aid taught in the wilderness context. Intended for people close to home or folks who want to be ready to help higher-trained providers.

Wilderness Advanced First Aid (WAFA). The WAFA course is designed for trip leaders and those traveling or working in remote areas who need a more extensive training program than the Wilderness First Aid course. This forty-hour course focuses on stabilization, treatment, and evacuation guidelines for patients in backcountry environments.

Wilderness First Responder (WFR). A WFR course is intended for non-medical professionals who are acting as a primary caregiver in a remote setting, who are employed or volunteering as wilderness guides, instructors and educators, Search and Rescue (SAR) team members, ski patrol, medical personnel for adventure races/events, missionaries, or wild-land firefighter medical team members. The 80-hour course, widely recognized as a professional standard in the outdoor industry, focuses on patient assessment, treatments (splints, wound care, spine injury management, managing environmental threats), and evacuation decisions.

Wilderness Upgrade for Medical Professionals (WUMP). This 40-hour course is designed for EMTs, nurses, physicians, physician assistants, other medical professionals, and medical students who want to learn to use their medical knowledge in a wilderness context. It focuses on patient assessment, management of injury, illness and environmental problems, and on evacuation decisions in remote and challenging environments with limited resources and gear.

Wilderness Emergency Medical Technician (WEMT). This course, taught to a national standard curriculum, combines wilderness medicine

During the NOLS Wilderness Medicine and Rescue Semester, students practice difficult medical scenarios in challenging terrain. WMI

with urban medical care practices into a single month-long program that includes clinical rotations helping to provide care for real patients. The WEMT is a professional credential used by ski patrol, SAR, ambulance, and other medical units.

Wilderness Medicine and Rescue Semester. The Wilderness Medicine and Rescue Semester is a unique blend of wilderness skills, medicine, rescue, leadership, and environmental studies curriculum offered only through WMI. The semester starts with an intensive four-week WEMT course, followed by nine field weeks consisting of backpacking, a rock climbing and rock rescue camp, and either river travel and rescue or winter travel with avalanche rescue. The semester is woven with themes of leadership, expedition behavior, communication, and decision-making, as well as wilderness evacuation, swiftwater, and rock rescue skills. This semester will provide you with the theoretical and practical foundations for a career in outdoor recreation, medicine, and rescue.

The Patient Assessment System (PAS)

The patient assessment system is the way we approach each and every patient to complete big picture detection of injury and illness and ensure quality care. Regardless of when your certification actually expires, rescuers should be able to demonstrate a professional PAS without the aid of

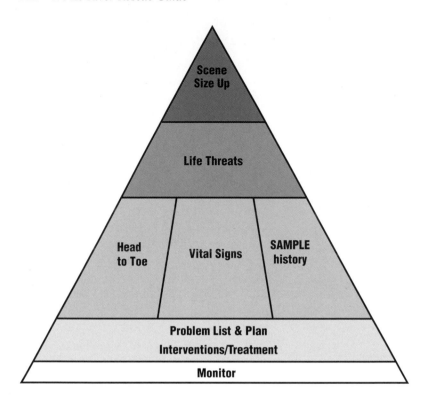

textbook or guide. Having a readily available first aid book is ideal, but we should avoid relying too heavily on this resource, as circumstances could be such that it isn't right there when you need it. Continue to practice the PAS on a regular basis with your team, so this essential skill is ready to employ in an emergency. If you are not doing a PAS run-through at least once a month, either on real patients or in a simulation, then you are arguably in a complacent state of preparation. Be creative, make training fun, and continue to raise the bar on one another.

Patient Care Documentation

"Meant is not said, said is not heard, heard is not understood, understood is not done."

Rescuers need to be able to communicate their patient's condition effectively. This leadership skill requires competency in both the written and verbal form. Documentation details the assessment and treatment of

SOAP Note

Name _____   **Date**_____

Location_____

Subjective/Summary/Story *(age, sex, chief complaint, OPQRST, MOI/HPI).*
_____
_____

Objective/Observations/Findings *(Describe position found. Describe injuries).*
_____
_____

Patient Exam _____
_____
_____

Vital Signs
Time _____   _____   _____
LOR _____   _____   _____
HR   _____   _____   _____
RR   _____   _____   _____
SCTM_____   _____   _____
BP   _____   _____   _____
Pupils _____   _____   _____
Temp _____   _____   _____

History
Symptoms_____
Allergies_____
Medications_____
Pertinent Medical History_____
Last Intake/Output_____
Events recent _____

Assessment *(List Problems)* _____
_____
_____

Plan *(Plan for each problem)*_____
_____

Anticipated problems _____
_____

the patient, as well as ensuring quality patient care, aiding in decision-making, and providing for continuity of care. Documentation needs regular updating as the rescuer continues to monitor their patient.

The SOAP acronym is commonly used for patient reports, and it stands for Summary, Observations, Assessment, Plan. It is a convenient and widely accepted format. Painting a clear picture is just as important as being brief and concise. Good SOAP reports can facilitate appropriate decisions about the urgency of a rescue. Poor SOAP reports can trigger unneeded urgency and risk.

Verbal SOAP reports are equally as important of a skill and require just as much practice as the written. Practice a full PAS once a month, then write out a complete SOAP report, then practice verbalizing that information out loud as if you were talking over the telephone. Boil down your message and eliminate as much extra verbiage as possible. "Ummms," "Ya knows," and other filler words add confusion to conversations and use up valuable time.

Basic Life Support: Cardio Pulmonary Resuscitation and Rescue Breathing

Knowledge of cardio-pulmonary resuscitation (CPR) and rescue breathing techniques is essential for all boaters. Remember not to focus on the expiration date of your certification card but rather on the rustiness of your knowledge base and ability to perform under pressure. Keep training. Keep testing yourself. Make the simulations challenging, fun, and measurable. Take ownership of your successes and shortfalls.

Recognize the benefits of training in professional-level CPR and BLS. Some CPR curriculums have simplified the instruction to Hands-Only CPR where no breaths are delivered to the patient at all. This can work well in an urban context where ambulances are likely to arrive on scene within ten minutes. For remote and backcountry responses, appreciate that oxygen therapy can play a vital role in the outcome of our patient care. For many wilderness context cardiac arrests, the patient's heart stopped beating secondary to hypoxia or low levels of oxygen in the system. Examples include avalanche burial, lightning strikes, and submersion or drowning incidents. Take a professional-level CPR course, and learn how to confidently approach a patient that is in cardiac arrest or having severe difficulty breathing.

CHAPTER 8

WHITEWATER SWIMMING

The Art and Science of Self-Rescue

"We're all in between swims."

Forget how good your swimming skills were two years ago and get back in the river and practice again. We want to go from being just a competent swimmer to a viable watercraft.

Without question, this is the one skill that we should all practice regularly. If you are not comfortable self-rescuing by swimming aggressively out of rapids and back to shore, then you should not be on scene for a river rescue scenario. Anyone within 10 feet of the riverbank should be in full personal protective equipment (PPE) and be prepared for an unintentional swim.

The only way to get better at whitewater swimming is to practice.

Practicing swims in fast-moving water instills the sense that we're skilled enough and confident enough to turn ourselves from mere swimmers into viable watercraft, just like rafts, canoes, or kayaks.

DEFENSIVE SWIMMING

If a swim occurs in a shallow, rocky river or in a large section of a rapid, a general guideline is to stay in a *defensive* swimming position until you can swim *aggressively* to shore. Defensive swimming means:

- Lie on your back with your feet downstream. Time your breathing with patience and keep your eyes open as much as possible.
- Maintain a horizontal position on the surface of the water by slightly arching your back.
- Keep your toes out of the water to help reduce the possibility of foot entrapment.
- If you see yourself going toward a hazard, such as a large wave or hole, be assertive. Stay on your back, and swim away from the object.
- Once you are out of the rapid, be assertive. Angle your head toward the closest, safest shore. Stay on your back, kick with your legs, and backstroke with your arms.

The defensive swim position, facing downstream with feet held high, helps prevent entrapments, and puts the legs in a position where they can readily absorb the impacts with rocks or debris.

Swimming in big water takes practice, strength, and technique.

- Kicking should be a constant 8-inch flutter with straight legs and use of gluteus (butt) muscles.
- Powerful, intentional, alternating back crawl strokes at a controlled rate can do more for propulsion than dozens of fluttery flailing strokes. Consider using two arms when steering or redirecting your angle across the current, and then transition back into smooth back crawl strokes.
- Do not stand up until you are in shallow water or a calm eddy and the potential for foot entrapment is minimal.

AGGRESSIVE SWIMMING

If a swim occurs in deeper water, or you are trying to catch a critical eddy, using an *offensive* or *aggressive* swimming position can be beneficial.

- Roll over on your stomach, and use the crawl stroke. Swim aggressively toward your intended target.
- Keep your head out of the water to ease breathing, and stay oriented to land and water features.
- Minimize knee and ankle injury by kicking with straight legs in a constant 8-inch flutter. This keeps your legs from dangling too deep in the water.
- Do not stand up until the potential for foot entrapment is minimized.

Aggressive swimming skills require frequent practice. Make this training fun and an anticipated aspect of your risk management culture.

Swiftwater Entries

Rescuers may need to enter the river as a rescue swimmer, or they may end up standing on a rock in the middle of a rapid. In many cases, easing into the water to begin your swim may not be an option. Rescuers may find they need to strategically jump into the main current. A good strong jump into mid-channel can also allow the rescuer to bypass part of a swim, saving her from washing downstream too fast or expending more energy than is necessary. There are critical techniques required to execute this potentially dangerous skill. If it is done incorrectly, the rescuer is in grave danger of serious injury, paralysis, or death. This skill needs to be practiced extensively under the coaching and guidance of a qualified instructor in a controlled environment in order to minimize the risk of injury.

Some critical elements of swiftwater entries are:

- Only consider swiftwater entries in water at least knee deep. Choose a launching point at knee level in the water or from a flat rock right at the surface. Entering from any higher out of the water may result in the swimmer going too deep and risking injury.
- Crouch low with legs staggered front to back and knees bent for takeoff.
- Raise arms straight backwards to shoulder height.
- Explode your jump outward aggressively, with the goal of hitting the water perfectly flat and with the head extended back, so your

eyes are looking out along the surface of the water. Do not drop your head like in a traditional dive, but rather keep your face up out of the water. Arms should extend straight out in front of you like a superhero flying.

- Aim for your padded torso to hit the water first by arching back and bringing arms and legs upward. Your PFD should hit the water first, *not your head or arms.*
- Do not flex your knees at all while in the air, or your legs will be exposed to serious injury.
- The goal is an aggressive entry with full extension of the body, getting as far away from the launching point as possible. Choose an angle of entry appropriate for reaching your target, hit the water with speed, and go right into aggressive crawl strokes.
- Try to maintain a visual of the patient or target as you launch into the water.

DO NOT DIVE INTO A RIVER

Swiftwater entries look a lot like a dive: They are not. *Never* dive into a river. Murky water, inconsistent river bottoms, and the dynamic nature of rivers that can change from season to season make it difficult to accurately assess the depth of the river. These factors make diving into a river extremely hazardous. Diving into shallow water is one of the leading causes of trauma in water-based accidents.

A swiftwater entry is not a dive. Arch your head and legs back, and try to "lead" with your PFD-padded torso. SACHA JACKSON

Never let your head or arms enter the water first. Your torso should be the first thing that hits the water. Additionally, your neck should be hyperextended, with your head reaching toward your back, rather than flexed or in a neutral position.

Ferry Angles

Crossing from one side of the river to the other requires identifying with the currents you are traveling through. Your head should be positioned upstream in both the defensive or aggressive swim positions when ferrying across a channel.

- Cross the channel at a 30- to 60-degree angle to the current in order to lose as little downstream progress as possible.
- Cross at a 90-degree angle to get to a general destination in the river faster. This can be effective when trying to move a few feet to the left or right in a technical rapid or when simply driving toward a different channel. It takes fewer strokes to get where you are going, but you travel farther downstream in the process.
- Practice ferrying across different channels while alternating between aggressive and defensive swim positions.

Crossing Eddy Lines

Swimming over eddy lines means transitioning across this interface of upstream and downstream current. This technique requires practice and skill.

- Cross the eddy line high in the eddy on the squeeze at a 90-degree angle. A 45-degree angle or flatter can result in getting rejected by the whirlpool action of the eddy line.
- Charge across the eddy line in an aggressive swim position, and reach with your upstream arm into the eddy water and pull yourself in. Reaching in with the downstream arm can expose the upstream shoulder to downstream currents and pull you back out into the main channel.
- Thrust your chest across the eddy line while kicking hard with your legs. Maintaining your limbs high on the surface allows for quicker crossing by distancing yourself from the deeper differential currents that may stop your progress.
- In powerful and wide eddy lines, it is sometimes better to cross farther downstream near the bottom of the eddy, so you can swim deeper into the pocket before recirculating back upstream.
- It's generally better to keep charging right across an eddy line, staying in the aggressive position throughout. Some powerful eddy lines

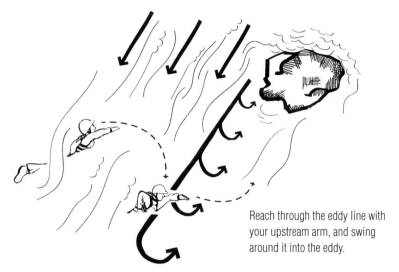

Reach through the eddy line with your upstream arm, and swing around it into the eddy.

with large whirlpools will want to turn your body as you cross the eddy line. When this happens, go with the rotation by executing one or more corkscrewing barrel rolls with your body. This can help flip you up over the eddy line, allowing you to proceed with aggressive crawl strokes to reach your target.

- Consider swimming up to the rock that makes the eddy after achieving your position below it. This can serve as an excellent opportunity for staging during a rescue or help break the river down into more manageable pieces. Use eddies and their rocks as locations for rest when training to navigate through large sections of terrain.

Rock Encounters

Exposed midstream rocks and boulders can serve as great resources during a river rescue and can effectively break down larger rapids into more manageable sections. Consider swimming into the eddy below when approaching them. If you encounter a rock from upstream, you have a few options:

- Bend your knees and use your feet to push off of the rock, and use rebound energy to redirect your swim.
- Time it to aggressively swim away when your body reaches the pillow, essentially body-surfing around it.
- Swim right up to the rock, and pull yourself up onto it. Practice swimming beneath or downstream of a rock and climbing onto it, to gain access to that point in the river.
- Develop the skills to identify undercut rocks. Absence of a pillow and absence of eddy water downstream of the rock are both possible

indicators that a rock could be undercut. Avoid these rocks by swimming aggressively away.

Swimming through Wave Trains and Holes

If you encounter large waves, try to swim away from them, since swimmers usually go through the wave instead of floating over them. If you can't swim away from a wave in time, try to catch a breath in its trough. Keep yourself oriented by looking around after you have taken a breath. The defensive swim position can be beneficial in timing breath sequence and for conserving energy until you can exit the rapid below. Consider throwing in powerful back crawl strokes to ferry yourself out of the wave train on one side or the other to make your swim more tolerable. In large

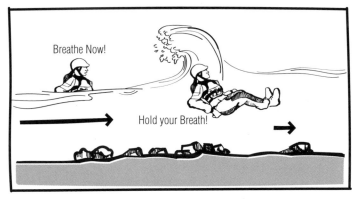

Even with PFDs, swimmers will go *through* large waves, not up and over them. Time your breathing, and try to relax until you resurface on the other side.

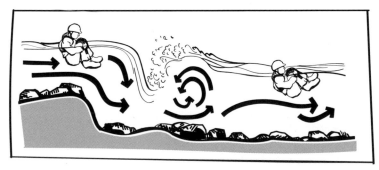

When swimming over steep holes and pourovers, tuck up into the cannonball position to protect your body and to avoid recirculation.

Some holes are swimmer friendly. Body surfing in the right hole can help develop a sense of recirculation and what to expect when the swim is unintentional.

waves the danger of foot entrapment is often lower, so an aggressive swimming position might be appropriate.

As a general principle, it is best to avoid swimming through holes, as possible outcomes will vary widely even in the same feature. If you encounter a hole, try to stay relaxed to conserve your energy. Since the water in a hole is moving in a circle, it is easy to become disoriented. Swimmers are sometimes flushed straight through holes by the current below the surface of the hole, and are pushed toward the river bottom. When this occurs the swimmer will continue to travel under the surface of the water and end up being washed out below the hole.

When swimming over steeper pourovers, holes, and ledges, it can be helpful to tuck up by bringing your knees up to your chin and dropping over in a cannonball position. In this position your legs are not as easily pulled down toward the river bottom, and the chance of foot entrapment can be reduced. There is also a better chance of flushing through the hole and resurfacing downstream of the boil line.

If you are not flushed out of the hole and are instead being recirculated as a swimmer, there are a couple of options for consideration:

- Feel for the direction of the flow or "foampile kick" and swim aggressively in that direction. This can often be planned during a scout by identifying each hole in the rapid and what to do if you end up in that particular one. Swim hard for the open corners of the hole. (See the River Features and their Anatomy section on page 94.) You may get surfed back up to the green water and pushed back underwater before you reach the corner. Each time you resurface, swim aggressively once again towards the open corner, and time your

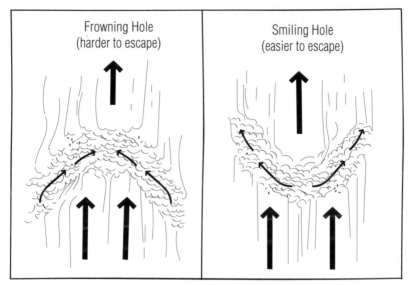

In general, the corners of a hole are the best place to escape its recirculation. Frowning holes, whose corners point upstream, are tougher to escape from than smiling holes, because the force of the current makes reaching the corners more difficult.

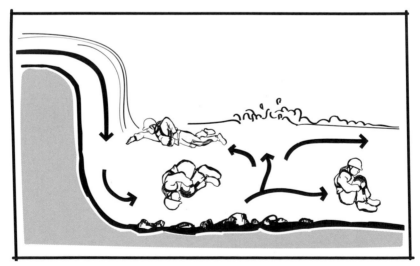

Escaping a powerful hole's recirculation can be difficult and may require several attempts. One option is to swim upstream towards the curtain of water in hopes of going deeper underwater where some undercurrents can aid escape. The swimmer balls up when first hitting the curtain of water but then opens up into an aggressive underwater swim once she reaches the undercurrents.

breathing intentionally. Exhibit good fear and concentration. Do not panic or overexert yourself.

- If you cannot get out of the corners, try changing your shape so a different current might catch your body. A swimmer can ball up to sink more for catching deeper currents or extend her arms and legs to try to surf to one of the edges along the surface.
- Another strategy is to swim directly upstream in the hole and penetrate the green water. This will likely send the swimmer down deep, so she can catch a current near the river bottom to be flushed out below the boil line. This is a riskier option since it may put her in contact with a riverbed that has entrapment potential.
- *Warning*: Some people will propose taking off a PFD as a last resort option when getting recirculated in a hole. The rationale is that you will become less buoyant and therefore flush out of the hydraulic. Generally speaking, this is a dangerous option, as it makes you less likely to survive after flushing out of the hole.

Swimming out of Boats

RAFTS
If you fall out of your raft, aggressively swim back and climb into it as quickly as possible. Perimeter lines that are tied tightly can assist a swimmer back into the boat. Swim hard for the boat, grab onto the perimeter line while kicking yourself up into a mantled handstand, and then throw a leg into the boat and climb in. If you don't have any momentum while trying to climb back into the raft, use the perimeter line to push yourself down deeper into the water to activate the buoyancy of your PFD, and then rocket back up to the surface while kicking hard to a mantled handstand. If the raft has oar frames, you may be able to climb on by grasping frame parts and hauling yourself up into the boat while kicking hard.

KAYAKS AND CANOES
If your boat flips and you swim out of it, try to hold on to your paddle and boat and get yourself to shore. Try to be on the upstream side of your boat and only hold on to it for extra flotation while kicking hard, angled towards the riverbank or to an eddy. If you feel that continuing to hold on to your gear, boat, or paddle is compromising your safety, then let go and self-rescue with appropriate technique for the terrain you are in.

Swimming with a Canoe or Raft Paddle
Swim to shore in an aggressive position while grasping the T-grip with your downstream hand. If you keep the paddle on the downstream side of your

When swimming with a kayak paddle, use the same motion as you would paddling your kayak.
MOE WHITSCHARD

body, it won't be continually forced into your body by the upstream current. Instead, it will travel in your portable eddy as you charge for shore. Grasping the paddle mid-shaft tends to result in bashing your face with the T-grip.

Swimming with a Kayak Paddle
Swimming with a kayak paddle can be much easier than swimming without any paddle at all. Use the kayak paddle to propel yourself through the water with leverage and power by stroking with it as you would if you were still inside your boat, but lying on your belly with your legs out behind you. Keep a constant straight-legged kick going with an 8-inch flutter. This is an effective technique, and if it's performed properly, it will result in a faster, more efficient swim, as well as better visibility and access to breathable air. As with all of these techniques, practice in low-stress settings will give you expertise you can depend on in more critical situations.

JUST KEEP SWIMMING
Becoming a rescue swimmer takes a combination of skill, precision, smarts, and confidence. This only comes with plenty of regular practice to verify your present abilities and comfort zones. Confidence is keyed into your acceptable level of risk and is ultimately determined through repetition of hard moves in easier rapids before moving into more advanced terrain. The best swiftwater rescue teams in the world are comprised of a collection of talented swimmers. Make it a goal to swim on a regular basis. Every boating trip you go on has the potential to allow you to squeeze in

NOLS instructors practicing swiftwater entries in early spring conditions in the Pacific Northwest. MOE WHITSCHARD

another ten or fifteen minute swim session to sharpen this essential and critical skill set. You cannot be a Class IV boater unless you can self-rescue in Class IV. Avoid complacency, and elevate the expectations of everyone in your group by modeling regular practice.

Strive to practice swimming on every boating trip.

■ A RIVER NARRATIVE: A PINNING IN ECUADOR

By Phil DeRiemer

My kayak was pinned flat to the riverbed. A submerged log that bridged the 4-foot wide slot I had just entered rested across my lap. The force of the river pounded into my back. My head was completely underwater. For the moment, though, my situation was stable—I had a small air pocket to breathe in, and my spray skirt was still in position, so no additional water was coming in and driving me deeper.

That log, bridging a 4-foot wide slot in a straightforward Class IV stretch of the Upper Misahualli in Ecuador, was totally unexpected. My wife, Mary, and I had run the stretch numerous times that season, and compared notes with a fellow guide who had been through the same slot just the day before. Even with so much local knowledge, we'd been careful, boat-scouting the slot before dropping in. But that log was just one more reminder that "safety" on a river doesn't exist; Mary told me later that even when standing directly above and looking down, it was not visible.

I had run the slot first. As I lay pinned, some of the group we were leading were waiting their turn in the staging eddy on river right just upstream of me, while others had begun portaging their boats on the opposite side of the river. Also on the river right shore was a group of locals who had stopped construction on a fish trap in the next channel over to watch us run through.

No more than 200 cfs flowed through the narrow gap, but it was still too much for me to free myself. To get out, I was going to need help. As I waited, I would occasionally thrust my arm up over my head to let the group know I was ready whenever they were—hoping it would be soon. I was told later that all that was visible was my hand breaking the surface. It seemed like an eternity before something began poking me through thundering water. I grabbed at what turned out to be a bamboo limb held by one of the locals on a large boulder above me. They pulled heartily, but the angle was wrong—all they could do from the boulder was pull me upward into the log. To free me, the pull would have to be from directly straight upstream. To communicate to them that their plan wasn't working, I let go of the limb. Three more times I was poked; three more times I rejected the pole. I continued to thrust my hand over my head to assure them I was still with them.

My hope was that they would switch tactics, and lower a rope to me. I was wearing a rescue vest and tow tether, and if the group could get me a line, perhaps I could clip in and get hauled out. I waited.

Some time later, a life jacket appeared in my air pocket. I thought it might be a person foolishly trying to shimmy out onto the slick log in the rushing current, but when I reached out to touch it, I found it was empty. I wasn't sure what they were up to, so, like the bamboo pole, I rejected their plan by letting go of the vest—and felt a rope slip through my fingers. They were doing just as I had hoped, and had attached a PFD to the end of the tagline to help me grab it.

Hoping they would try a second time, I very carefully unclipped my cow tail from the front of my vest and held it at the ready. As I sat there, tense and expectant, the baseball cap I wore under my helmet flushed out. My air pocket instantly diminished, but at the same time, the vest appeared again.

I found the rope, clipped it, and let go.

Almost immediately I felt the pull of the tow tether attached to the back of the vest— they were hauling me out. The boat and I began to move back upstream. I was on my way out! But in almost the same instant I felt the boat tumbling out of control, like they had pulled me free and then just let me go. On my belly, head upstream and still in my boat, I flushed over something smooth, clutched it (it turned out to be the very log I had been pinned under), grabbed a quick breath, and kicked the boat off my lower body.

However, the group didn't know why I had stopped. They had been lowering me downstream under control, and now, worried that they were holding me up, did the only thing they could think of to free me: They let go of the rope. But to no avail; when I let go of the log, I only traveled a short distance before the rope went tight again—it had snagged on the log.

The rope coming tight pulled at the anchor point on the back of my vest. The tension flipped me over onto my back, holding me head up with feet downstream. I could see Mary in a nearby eddy. She had swum to a midstream boulder to set up the tagline, and then leaped into the eddy when I was pulled free. Mary was in an eddy close by. She had swum to midstream to set up the tag line, and then leaped into an eddy to see if she could reach me. I pulled the quick release on my chest harness. Mary extended her arm as far out as she could from the safety of the eddy. I swam to her outstretched arm and swung safely into the eddy with her. Elapsed time, twelve to fifteen minutes!

The rescue succeeded for a number of reasons. Some were mere chance: The warm water of the tropics prevented me from going into hypothermia, I hadn't been injured when I was pushed into the log, and the locals lent a hand with pulling me out. However, our team's preparation was critical. I was wearing a rescue vest, my rescuers were skilled and knowledgeable, and finally, I knew what they were trying to accomplish and had the experience and training to help them help me.

Phil DeRiemer owns and operates DeRiemer Adventure Kayaking with his wife, Mary. He has the first descent of the Futaleufu River in Chile and participated in early descents of the Grand Canyon of the Stikine and Middle Fork of the San Joaquin. ◾

CHAPTER 9

WADING AND SHALLOW WATER CROSSINGS

Traversing the Riverbed with Intent

WADING

Pause for a moment before deciding to wade a shallow river. In many circumstances, swimming can be a lower risk option than wading, because foot entrapment is less likely. When trying to get to a precise spot such as an entrapped patient or boat, however, sometimes wading is your best option. It also may be the quickest way to get to them, so get proficient at this skill long before you think you might need it.

Novice rescuers need to spend hours practicing wading techniques under the guidance of seasoned experts. This gives each person a feel for what conditions they can wade alone, at what point they need to enlist a team, and what terrain requires a swim rather than a wade. Practical experience develops both the kinesthetic skills and the judgment needed for future river crossings.

TRAINING CONSIDERATIONS

Practicing on land is an effective, low-exposure strategy for fine-tuning mechanics. As comfort increases, you should attempt different techniques in a variety of currents and depths to become familiar with the strengths and limitations of each crossing method. Begin practicing skills in water no higher than your knees before going into deeper currents. Strive for efficiency in movement and communication before entering more challenging terrain.

Train in challenging and realistic sections of a river with a good runout and with appropriate risk management. In appropriate conditions, test the limitations of your techniques by wading out until your team is broken up by the current. In other words, wade until you blow out and swim. Training to failure helps rescuers understand when to call stop in a real event. Understanding what is and isn't possible is an underlying theme in

NOLS instructors train in wading techniques in the Frank Church Wilderness, Idaho.
MOE WHITSCHARD

effective training. Progress toward the goal of "go until you blow" as comfort level and ability allow.

Foot entrapment is a significant concern when practicing wading. Most wading techniques require rescuers to face upstream, as it is a more natural way to resist forces that are trying to knock you over. Foot entrapment while you are facing upstream can be exceptionally dangerous; if you fall over backwards, you likely have no way of stabilizing your own airway and rescue attempts may not be quick enough. Plan in advance what steps you'll take in the event of a foot entrapment during this practice procedure and reinforce the following critical principles:

- Scout effectively, identifying potential hazards including holes, strainers, and undercut rocks. Plan your route so that it includes midstream eddies as potential rest stops during your traverse. Decide where to swim should the wade fail, and identify key eddies for consideration. The run-out below the crossing should be free of major rapids and hazards. To gauge water speed, throw a stick into the main current, and walk next to it on the bank. In thigh-deep water, most people cannot cross if the current is moving faster than they can walk. All team members should be comfortable with the location prior to committing to wading.

- Establish upstream and downstream spotters. Upstream spotters should alert the team to incoming boat traffic and debris. Downstream spotters are placed to assist swimmers if need be, and can include both rescuers with throw bags and tethered, or "live bait," rescue swimmers.

- During the actual crossing, be sure to traverse the riverbed intentionally. Do not allow the current to pull you downstream while standing on your feet; downstream momentum can quickly turn into a foot entrapment. If footing is compromised and a fall is inevitable, don't fight the process. Instead, just allow the fall and swim back to shore. Trying to stop a fall can lead to foot entrapment. If the run-out is really shallow, use a defensive swim position by staying on your back with your toes in the air. The default swim plan should be an aggressive swim back to shore to minimize time in the water and exposure to hazards. Avoid arresting your downstream progress by standing up in moving water—especially when deeper than knee height.

- PFDs can create hazards of their own in deeper wading-depth water. When the rescuer reaches depths up to her PFD, its buoyancy will start to pick her up and skip her downstream. It can look as if she is jumping backward across the moon, a motion that exacerbates the chances of foot entrapment. To prevent this dangerous situation, pull up your feet immediately and begin swimming for shore. As a spotter, watch your team carefully, and if you see this happening, blow your whistle immediately, and tell them to swim.

- Set an appropriate rescuer tone. The basic principle in all techniques is to maintain stability by employing intentional foot placement, solid balancing, and fluid weight transference. While re-establishing foot placement, focus attention on the move, and avoid looking at the final destination. Once your footing is solid, you can spot your target, offer eye contact to the patient, or speak with people on shore. While you are moving, however, focus completely on the move, so time isn't wasted falling and recovering. In challenging terrain where footing is difficult, keep momentum going until you get to a more secure place.

- Establish expectations for communication while wading, and keep it simple, clear, and minimal. In multi-person techniques, communication becomes a key factor in the performance outcome.

- Water clarity affects your ability to see the riverbed when assessing the depth. Clarity is affected by turbidity (suspended solids in muddy or glacier-fed rivers), depth, waves or rapids, and vegetative tannins. A river can be opaque and shallow or opaque and deep.

- Riverbed composition determines the type of footing one can expect when wading a river. Sand, silt, or gravel riverbeds can offer good footing. Large river cobbles, ranging from softball- to basketball-size, can create unstable footing. Submerged boulders present a foot entrapment hazard. Submerged boulders that you can hear moving downriver indicate an unstable riverbed. Muddy riverbeds (commonly seen in canyons) can trap waders in awkward positions, or cause them to start sinking.

- Use appropriate technique. Solo wading techniques are fast but provide less support in strong currents. Wading as a group is a much more stable arrangement than going it alone. In general, techniques that face across the river (versus upstream) are easier and faster to execute, but are more difficult to reverse if the conditions are found to be too challenging. Facing downstream is not recommended, because the current can buckle your knees and cause you to lose balance.

- Wade into the current, and work to keep the group oriented upstream to the current vector, not necessarily toward the riverbank. Keep moving. Standing still wastes energy and increases risks. Avoid staring at the river. Moving water can be mesmerizing and can interfere with balance. Look upstream and watch for incoming debris. Take small steps and move one foot at a time. Move slowly and weight the foot carefully. If using a stick or paddle, move it first to feel for any obstacles or deeper channels.

WADE

The key elements of a successful shallow water crossing are stopping, analyzing, decision-making, and skill in executing the chosen technique. The WADE principle provides a mechanism to focus attention on the important elements of judging shallow water crossings.

WADE stands for:

Wait	Don't rush into the river before a full evaluation can occur. Go slow to go fast. Consider establishing upstream and downstream spotters when possible.
Analyze	Scout the rapid, and determine target zone, hazards, and best route options. Plan for and be aware of environmental conditions.
Decide	Can the river be waded effectively? Do the conditions match the group's abilities and physical and emotional states? If yes, what crossing technique will be used? If no, make alternative plans.
Execute	Devise a crossing plan, communicate how the plan will be executed, and begin wading.

Wading Techniques

ONE-PERSON HAND SURF

When a paddle, a stick, or other rescuers aren't readily available, a rescuer may need to do a solo wade with no resources at all. Face upstream, and traverse into the current with legs staggered front to back. Place your hands in the water for stability and to make subtle strokes to maintain your position.

LINE ASTERN

One person line astern. Use a canoe or kayak paddle to establish a tripod base of support, or find a sturdy stick about 6 feet in length. Three points of contact are more stable than two. Keep legs wide and face upstream. With canoe or raft paddles, invert the paddle with the T-grip down. By placing the T-grip down, you have less surface area in the current, and it will be much easier to relocate the paddle to a new position. With kayak paddles you have no choice but to place a blade into the water; slice the blade into the water so it is parallel to the current, and then turn it sideways to the current for a solid purchase on the riverbed floor. Once balance is set, twist the blade to relieve pressure and relocate to a new position on the riverbed. Use caution, aiming for small gains on each new placement to avoid challenging balance situations.

Multi-person line astern. Additional rescuers can line up behind the primary wader and create a single file line where each rescuer stands in the

One-person line astern wading.

Multi-person line astern.

eddy of the person in front of them. Support one another by grabbing on to the lapels of the PFD in front of you. Move efficiently in shallower water by traveling in unison. When currents get stronger or deeper, you may want to stagger your progress. Have the lead wader move first and get re-established while the remaining rescuers provide support without moving their feet. Once the leader has a new position and has created a new eddy, the remaining rescuers can move in behind her. Line astern works well with one to five rescuers. Placing taller, wider, and stronger people up front can help in creating a bigger eddy for the rescuers behind them, but consider placing a smaller person in front if they have more competence in the technique.

TENSION TRIANGLE

When a paddle or stick isn't readily available, the tension triangle becomes a good consideration. Two or three people face each other, one facing downstream and the other one or two facing upstream. Take hold of one another's lapels, and create stability and tension by leaning into each other as you cross. Extend one leg straight behind you to create a solid base of support. Move in unison through easier terrain, and consider staggering your progress in more challenging water. The upstream person (preferably the largest member of the team) moves first, then the downstream rescuers step into the resulting eddy. The downstream position is also good for a nervous group member; she can't see downstream but rather is face to face with the upstream person, receiving instructions and reassuring feedback.

A 2-person tension triangle.

A 3-person tension triangle.

WEDGE

This technique is sometimes referred to as the pyramid, but consider using one syllable words when possible to make conversation easier over the roar of whitewater. Ideally, the wedge is executed with at least six people: a point person with two behind her and three people in a third row form a triangle that points into the current. The point person at the tip of the triangle should use a stick or pole for added support, just as in the line astern technique. The

The wedge wading technique requires a strong and skilled leader up front. This isn't always the biggest person in your group.

wedge creates a large portable eddy that can be helpful in several scenarios. For instance, moving in just upstream of a foot-entrapped patient can calm the water and make releasing the foot much easier. A wedge could also collect a stranded patient midstream and transport her back to shore by placing her in the center. If the patient is injured and cannot walk, she could be transported back to shore using the wedge by holding on to the patient's lapels and floating her behind the rescuers.

CHAIN

The chain technique is performed by a team holding hands and/or linking arms. Variations include facing upstream and sidestepping across perpendicular to the current, or facing the opposite bank and crossing parallel to the current. This technique is effective when crossing shallow waters with uniform riverbed composition, such as a shoal or small cobblestone.

POLE CHAIN

This is a variation of the chain technique, using a long pole or stick instead of linking arms. The pole needs to be 10 feet or longer to be an aid in this technique. Such poles are not easy to come by, but when available can allow rescuers to be bridged across deeper channels even if they have momentary loss of contact with the riverbed bottom. The pole chain has been effective in strong currents almost chest deep. This is a surprisingly strong technique and can be effective with more people and a longer pole.

The chain wading technique is an excellent consideration for fast travel across a shallow, uniform river bed such as a cobble or sand bar.

LADDER

The ladder is a good consideration when moving in unison poses too much risk of blowing out, as is sometimes the case when crossing a section filled with various-sized rocks or ledges. This can be done effectively with three or more rescuers. The first rescuer steps into the current and stabilizes her

A fire department swiftwater rescue team practices the ladder technique for wading across a river.

position. The next rescuer moves through the eddy created by the first rescuer and gets into position on the far side of her. The third (and fourth and fifth) rescuer now travels in the eddy behind both the first and second rescuer to get to her position in line. The first rescuer then travels behind the entire line to work out even farther into the current, and the whole process repeats.

Wading is a powerful tool for the river rescuer. Develop your abilities and experience base with the different crossing techniques by getting plenty of practice in various terrain. Expand your knowledge of the environment and your familiarity with the power of moving water.

■ A RIVER NARRATIVE: WHITEWATER SELF DEFENSE

By Kent Ford

While filming our instructional river rescue film, *Whitewater Self Defense*, I had the opportunity to do a lot of swimming in the river. We backed up each shooting location with talented rescuers and throw bags in downstream eddies. After dozens of swims with attempted throw bag rescues, I gained greater appreciation of the risk of rope entanglement on the river. Once, as I demonstrated how to swim with a kayak, a throw rope got tangled around my neck! Later that same day, another line wrapped around my wrist.

Most paddlers I know have seen all the throwing mistakes: letting go of the entire rope and watching the whole thing sail into the river, catching a tree with the rope instead of getting it out to the swimmer, getting pulled into the river instead of pulling the swimmer to shore, and knocking down innocent bystanders and creating more patients. We did a humorous section of the instructional video reenacting these types of blunders. This footage can be seen at performancevideo.com.

The lesson of all this? Throw rope precautions are important: Have a knife readily available, and do not tie into the rope in any way—better to let go and lose the rope than to bring it tight around your friend's neck.

Kent Ford's highly acclaimed books, videos, and instruction have made him one of the most recognized paddlers worldwide. He has spent more than twenty years racing, coaching, and teaching recreational boating to all levels of paddlers. ■

Belays should be performed with the primary rope on the downstream side to ease escape from the system if needed.

around your body from the upstream side; doing so requires the rope to run over your body should you attempt an escape.

Friction bends/terrain belays. Using friction bends around trees and rocks can lessen the load on the rescuer considerably. Simply walk the taut line around a solid, inanimate object to minimize force on the body. These can be quick and useful substitutes to a body belay when available. Remember to "give" as much as possible to ease the force on the swimmer.

Backup belays. Additional personnel in the vicinity of a rescuer making a throw bag toss can assist by giving a backup belay. Get behind the thrower and grab the lapels of her PFD and stabilize her upright posture. In some cases the backup belayer may want to also grab the rope to get four hands on it instead of just two.

SPECIFIC THROWING TECHNIQUES

Underhand throws. When standing on relatively flat and predictable terrain, underhand throws can offer the highest probability of an accurate, full-extension throw. Swing your throwing arm straight back behind in the vertical plane. Stop when your hand is at shoulder height behind, and pause for a second before throwing forward. This momentary pause allows for a more intentional throw. Swing your arm straight forward and release the bag when your hand is at shoulder height in front of you.

Overhand and sidearm throws. Underhand tosses are not always an option. Standing in waist-deep water, throwing from a raft, or needing

There is an art to the backup belay. A hand on the primary belayer's PFD can keep him upright, and getting four hands on the rope provides additional security. Keep your eyes on the patient.

Practice belay and rope management technique on a frequent basis. Cracks in slick river rocks can be great footholds to support a belay.

This throw bag team is well set up to handle the weight of multiple "big fish" on the line.

to clear a large rock in front of you are times you might consider an overhand toss.

Classic overhand throw. With smaller throw bags that have ¼-inch rope, consider using a baseball-style throwing technique. Finish your throw with your hand pointing at your target.

Straight arm overhand throw. Larger throw bags with ⅜-inch rope are heavy and can cause injury if you try to throw them like a baseball. Minimize articulating your wrist, elbow, and shoulder when throwing heavy objects by keeping your arm straight and throwing over the top. Finish your throw with your hand pointing at your target.

Sidearm tosses. Experiment with sidearm tosses to determine if they are within your acceptable level of risk or not. Many find the sidearm toss to be fast and powerful but lacking in overall accuracy.

Full bag of water technique. After the bag is thrown, a quick retrieval and a second attempt may be required if the first toss was unsuccessful, or an additional swimmer is coming through the rapid. Consider using the full bag of water technique or a coil technique. For the full bag of water technique, step on the end of the rope, and quickly stack the rope at your feet as you pull in the bag. When the bag arrives at you, it will be full of water and ready for a fast second toss. The weight of the water in the bag will aid its flight and it can often reach distances of 20 feet or more. This is a slower method than throwing coils, as you have to pull the bag all the way back to shore before you can make the second attempt. Be mindful of the rope stack at your feet, as it could pose a potential threat for grabbing onto a foot or ankle.

Throwing coils. Throwing coils can work as a backup, or as your primary throw—especially when working on a narrow section of river with potential entanglements on the far shore. You can meter out the exact length you think you'll need, and keep the remaining rope in the bag. To make coils, either make alternating bights of rope from one side of your hand to the other (butterfly coils), or smooth continuous loops (mountaineer's coils). When making mountaineer's coils, twist the rope with your hand as you go to take out natural rope kink. Whichever method you choose, coil the rope in your throwing hand rather than transferring it from your non-throwing hand. This will minimize tangling. Make coils 12 to 18 inches in length. Throw coils in a smooth and firm action rather than fast and jerky. These tips will help keep the coils quiet and un-tangled.

Off-hand throws. Occasionally we can find ourselves in the predicament where making a throw attempt with our strong arm is not an option. Practice making all of the above tosses with your off hand, and determine which are viable for you. Focus on the basics—step in opposition and follow through pointing at your target. This can also be helpful with some advanced techniques seen in the Foot Entrapment section on page 36.

VECTORING THE LINE

A second rescuer can expedite the retrieval of a swimmer after a successful throw bag toss by *vectoring the line*. Use a hand or clip a sling to the line, and walk down the shoreline toward the swimmer. This sideways pulling shortens the retrieval distance and can also aid in avoiding a pendulum through obstacles.

Vectoring a line can help get a swimmer to shore when avoiding downstream hazards or when wide eddies create unpredictable currents.

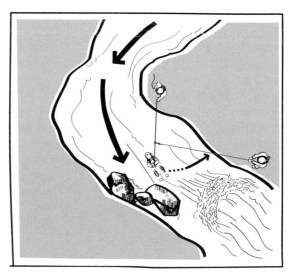

Swimmers should place the rope over the upstream shoulder and face away from the belayer.

Receiving the Rope as a Swimmer

If a rope is thrown to you while you are swimming, grab onto the rope itself and not the bag. If the rope lands several feet away from you, aggressively swim toward it. Once you have it, place it over your upstream shoulder, and hold with both hands. With the line over your upstream shoulder, your body will naturally assume the correct ferry angle, and you'll be able to breathe much more easily. Keep your hands close to your chest, your face up, and your feet downstream. Remember not to tie or wrap the rope around any part of your body. Once the rescuer has pulled you to a safe place, you can let go of the rope. If you feel that you are being put in greater jeopardy by continuing to hold on to the rope, let go.

Practice, Practice, Practice

Beware of the snake, and only throw a rope when necessary. Throw it deliberately to minimize entrapment risks. Although you may not use this tool often, it is very important to become proficient at this skill set. You are only as good as your next throw. Don't assume your technique is as sharp as it was last year or even your last trip. Keep throwing, and keep teaching others how to effectively mitigate the risks involved with ropes.

■ A RIVER NARRATIVE:
BLOWING UP COMPLACENCY

By Kristin and Sean Bierle

The Rio San Pedro is one of the largest rivers in the famous Lake District of Chile, with turquoise water and enormous waves. We first ran the Rio San Pedro in 2003, while working as guides for another river outfitter, and were excited to repeat the trip with students from the Alzar School when we visited the area in 2010.

We anticipated that a trip down the Class IV, remote San Pedro would be a highlight of the students' experience in Chile. However, like almost every river in Chile, the San Pedro has been threatened by hydroelectric dam projects in recent years, and we sent our small advance team to do pre-expedition reconnaissance. One of our Chilean paddling instructors had heard that the Rio San Pedro's dam project had indeed started, so we squeezed a scouting run into our busy schedule.

On the way to the put-in, we stopped in at the construction office for the dam. It was a good thing we did! The crew was blasting with dynamite that day and downriver travel was prohibited (not to mention a bad idea). We noted dates we could access the river with our students and the advance team returned to the river later, on a day with no blasting.

From our previous visit to the river and scant info from online guides, we knew of two crux Class IV rapids, "El Reloj" and "Toro," which we scouted before running successfully. Then, we cruised downstream quickly, and through the massive dam construction site. As we passed, we discussed our sadness to lose this gem. Having made it through "El Reloj" and "Toro," we were a bit complacent, assuming the remaining rapids were all minor.

Instead, we blindly paddled into a very large, very difficult Class IV rapid that had been created by rocks dynamited into the river. Several of us flipped. We made it out OK, but our minds raced . . . What if the rapid hadn't flushed into a pool, but into a logjam or sieve? It was a wake-up call.

When we returned to the river with students about three weeks later, our group scouted "El Reloj," "Toro," and "The Dam Rapid." The rapid had changed again in that short time period, with more rocks added to the riverbed from continued blasting. The students negotiated it successfully, and the trip down the river was a peak experience for them.

This episode cemented a few key concepts in how we as a school manage risk in dynamic whitewater environments. Most importantly, we strive to avoid complacency as part of our risk management training for all students and staff. On the Rio San Pedro, we saw how easy it is to lose focus on the river. In response, we seek to create a culture of challenging complacency, especially at the end of a river trip or the school year, when it becomes all too easy to "take it easy."

Kristin and Sean Bierle are the founders of the Alzar School (www.alzarschool.org), a semester leadership school. The school continues to lead expeditions in Chile each semester. A magnitude 8.8 earthquake off the coast of Chile in February 2010 paused construction on the San Pedro hydroelectric project indefinitely. ■

CHAPTER 11

RESCUE SWIMMING

Rescue Swims: No Tether

Rescue swimming is high risk by nature. For rescue swimming to be a viable option, it must be practiced regularly in challenging terrain. Rescue swimming is one of the most dangerous aspects of river rescue.

Rescuers can perform simple, fast, and effective contacts with patients in trouble by simply swimming out to them. This may be necessary when the patient is unable to hold on to a throw rope or there is not enough time to set up a tethered rescue swim. It can be performed without any additional equipment other than standard PPE. Without a tether, the rescue swimmer has the flexibility to choose the time and place of contact with

Here a rescuer stands on the ready for a tethered rescue swim. On belay and in position, he can quickly execute a swiftwater entry into the river and retrieve an unresponsive floating patient.

A tethered swim can be the quickest way to rescue an entrapped patient, but it requires practice and crystal clear understanding between rescuer and belayers.

the patient and can chase after them if necessary. You will need to either swim the patient back to shore or receive a throw bag from a belay team. Use the cross-chest carry rescue technique to swim the patient back to shore or bear hug them from behind and await boat support. When receiving a throw bag, remember to place it over your upstream shoulder for a smooth pendulum swing back to shore.

CONTACT RESCUES: THE COMBATIVE PATIENT
Making contact with a patient in the water can be extremely risky for a rescue swimmer. Patients who appear catatonic or reserved can quickly become panicked and combative when the rescue swimmer makes contact. Fear can cause a patient to disconnect from reality, and the patient may not even realize that she has climbed on top of the rescuer and driven her below the water. Do not take this personally. The panicked patient may not see a rescuer as a human being so much as a potential life raft that will provide her with easier access to oxygen molecules. Keep your eyes on the patient as you approach her, and shout to let her know you are arriving. Look for signs of aggression and combative behavior as you deliver clear commands and instructions. Tell her to stay calm, that you are there to help, and that she needs to listen to you. Be ready to lock down your patient's movements with an "in-water restraint" by grabbing the lapels of her PFD from behind while driving your knees into her shoulders.

If the patient begins to aggressively climb on top of you, there are several defensive steps you can try:

Swim away. Teach the patient to self-rescue by letting her chase you back to shore. Face her as much as possible, as you continue to stay out of her reach. Coach her to keep swimming toward you and to kick with her legs.

Water shield. If you don't have time to swim away, consider pushing a sheet of water directly into the patient's face. This will take oxygen from the patient, and she may turn her face away from you to get another breath. As she turns away, be ready to aggressively lock her down with the in-water restraint technique described above.

Redirect energy. If there is no time to try either of the first two suggestions, you may have to engage physically with the patient. You are there to rescue, not injure, the patient, so try to avoid hitting her. As she lunges toward you, take her momentum and redirect it by grasping her opposite arm and turning her quickly around, and then use the in-water restraint technique.

Pull patient underwater. If the patient climbs on top of you, redirect her momentum by twisting and shoving her head under the surface of the water. If you no longer present yourself as a potential life raft, the patient may let go of you and swim for air. As she releases, swim away aggressively, try to approach her from behind as she resurfaces, and use the in-water restraint.

CONTACT RESCUES: SPINAL PRECAUTIONS AND UNRESPONSIVE PATIENTS

Patients floating unresponsive and heads-down may also have a spinal injury, and precautions should be taken using one of the following methods:

Crossover roll. Reach across and grab the patient's opposite wrist and pull down through the water to roll the patient quickly around the axis of her spine. As she re-surfaces, lock her down with the in-water restraint technique, and use your forearms to stabilize her head and spine in a neutral position.

Arm sandwich roll. For patients without a PFD, raise the patient's arms against her head and clamp them together as you roll her over. Continue to squeeze her arms against her head with one arm cradled underneath them to maintain a neutral spine position. Wait for a throw bag from shore or boat assistance, or begin swimming towards shore.

PFD twist. Cross your arms and grab the PFD lapels of the face-down patient. Twist your arms back to normal resting position to roll the patient quickly around the axis of her spine. As she re-surfaces, lock her down in the in-water restraint position, and use your forearms to stabilize her head and spine in a neutral position.

Tethered Rescue Swims

Tethered rescue swims—also known as "live bait" rescues—make getting the patient back to shore considerably easier than untethered swims. However, a tethered swim introduces other risks to the equation: The rescuer is not only in the turbulent water with a potentially combative swimmer, but also has a rope attached to her back that could present real entanglement danger. Tethered rescue swims require regular practice. They also require a type V rescue PFD with a releasable harness that allows a rescuer to free the rope from the rescue belt on her back by pulling a release buckle near her chest. (See the PPE section on page 71 for more information on type V rescue PFDs.) Rescuers should never tie directly into a rope without a releasable harness. It is important to read the PFD manufacturer's instructions and receive professional training before attempting tethered rescue swims. It is not advisable to retrofit an existing PFD with a releasable harness, or attempt a homemade version. Considerable amounts of time and money have been invested in the research and design of these vests, but there are still several risk factors involved with using them.

CUSTOM-FIT THE HARNESS
Rescue PFDs are often sold with extra webbing that runs through the harness itself to accommodate wearers of various sizes. Get fully suited in

Many elements come into play when executing a successful tethered rescue swim. Focus on the basics, so this advanced skill set can be achieved with minimal risk.

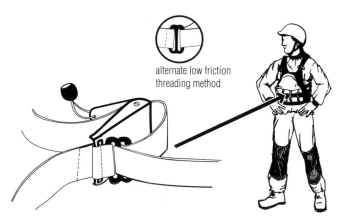

alternate low friction
threading method

Consider threading your releasable rescue harness differently depending on the situation and on the weight of the rescuer. The higher the load pulling on the harness, the more friction needs to be created in the threading of the webbing. For high-load situations such as a tethered rescue swim, thread your harness as shown in the main drawing. The alternate low-friction method works well for low-load situations. Either way, finish threading the plastic buckle as shown.

your PPE with all the layers you could potentially wear on your torso. Put the PFD on, and thread it per the manufacturer's recommendations. Make a mark on the excess webbing about 6 inches beyond the buckle. Use a hot knife to cut the webbing at an angle along this mark. You can also cut it with scissors, melt the edge with a flame, then quickly roll it with a round bar or pipe to flatten out the melted edge. If the tail is too long, the system will not release quickly.

THREADING THE RESCUE BELT
The manufacturer's recommended setup of the buckle above includes fully threading it through the metal tri-glide as shown. This creates a friction system in which the metal tri-glide takes the full load of the rescuer, and the plastic release buckle simply holds the tension. This arrangement is particularly effective for high loads, such as using the rescue PFD to anchor a belayer to the riverbank (see page 168). Some rescuers find this is too much friction for tethered rescue swims and will instead thread the harness as shown in the inset above.

RELEASE OF RESCUE BELT
Learning how easily your rescue PFD releases when needed is critical information in using one of these tools. Test how well your PFD releases by swimming into the current on a belayed tether while attempting to cross to the other side. Have the belay team arrest your progress when you are deep

in the current to simulate the sensation of the rope getting stuck on a rock and requiring you to release. Pull the toggle or the end of the webbing to release the harness. Experiment with different situations in various terrains to determine how well your harness releases depending on the application.

GETTING ON BELAY

Being placed on a tethered rescue swim is comparable to being on belay for a rock climb. Have an intentional conversation with your belayer about the setup for this system. Attach a locking carabiner to the ring on the back of the PFD (or to the webbing itself if there is no ring). Be sure to lock the carabiner so that it does not travel around on the harness and accidentally clip a point that is not releasable. Do not clip into a rescue PFD with a non-locking carabiner. The belayer should double-check the rescue swimmer's PPE and harness setup before declaring, "You're on belay."

EXECUTING THE TETHERED RESCUE SWIM

Choose a good location to enter the river. The rescue swimmer will ideally enter the river in the same current the patient is traveling in to make the timing easier to estimate. Anticipate the path of the pendulum, and determine if there will be any encounters with rocks or other hazardous features. Consider having the rescue swimmer positioned upstream of the belay team to allow for more time to swim to the patient before the pendulum starts to bring him back.

Use a swiftwater entry to launch into the river and swim to your patient. A common mistake is to jump too early, which forces the rescue swimmer to spend valuable energy swimming against the current while

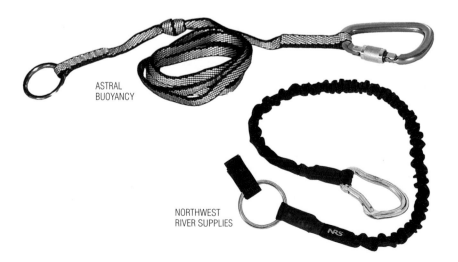

ASTRAL
BUOYANCY

NORTHWEST
RIVER SUPPLIES

awaiting the patient's arrival. Jumping early also tends to drag the rope downstream and can result in the rescuer and patient becoming entangled after they make contact. It is sometimes better to leave almost a little late and have the rope pay out cleanly behind you.

When you reach the patient, apply the in-water restraint technique, and quickly tap your head a couple of times to indicate to the belay team that they no longer need to pay out rope but can instead start managing the rope to effectively swing you to shore.

A backup belayer should be on hand to help with the heavy load of two people on the end of the line. Belayers should get into position facing downstream and sitting on the ground with feet propped up against natural features for stability, and should manage excess rope in a stack on the downstream side of their bodies. The backup belayer can either hold onto the primary belayer's PFD lapels, or onto the rope itself. Backup belayers can also communicate how much rope is left in the stack.

OPTIONAL TOW TETHERS

Rescue PFDs can be further customized by adding a tow tether. These serve as an extension of the ring on the back of the harness and allow the rescuer to use the PFD in other specialized ways. While they can be used for tethered rescues, the most common use for the tow tether is for a rescue kayaker or canoeist to tow an abandoned kayak/canoe to shore by clipping into the bow or stern loop. A tow tether could also be used as an anchor point for belay (see the next page) or as part of a tensioned diagonal. Tethers do present a risk of entrapment, particularly if there is a non-locking carabiner on the end of them. Consider swapping out all non-locking carabiners for locking versions to mitigate this risk. Just swimming in the water with a tow tether that is not in use introduces a large loop in the water that can get hung up on any number of things. Unless you are whitewater kayaking or canoeing, you really do not need one of these systems. Use low-friction threading of the rescue harness when towing.

ANCHOR POINT FOR BELAY

Rescue PFD harnesses can also be used to secure your belay position better in steep and challenging terrain or when belaying tethered rescue swims if a backup belayer is unavailable. Use a tow tether, your rescue belt/flip line, or a throw bag as an extension from yourself to a solid fixed anchor point or to a backup belayer that is on the next ledge system above you.

V-LOWERS

V-lowers are another application for rescue PFDs and are used when a rescuer must be lowered down to a specific point in the river to access a patient. This is a very difficult technique to execute even in the most ideal conditions, and it requires a talented belay team on both shores with excellent communication and rope management skills to successfully accomplish. V-lowers are most effective in fast-moving flat water such as in canal rescues or in Class I rapids. In rapids greater than Class II, this technique is often too dangerous, as the rescuer's visibility and hearing are compromised significantly.

The releasable rescue harness on a type V rescue PFD makes an excellent belay anchor point. This can be helpful in challenging situations where footing is less than ideal. Be sure to position yourself so that the anchor and load form a straight line to avoid getting pulled off balance.

■ A RIVER NARRATIVE: DANCE WITH THE DRAGON

By Marty McDonnell

If you saw a conspicuous crack in the window of a jet plane you were about to board, what would you do? Would you warn others of the apparent danger? Would you refuse to get on the plane? If the window failed at 32,000 feet, you and everyone aboard might get sucked out. But what if you were wrong and overreacted? Who are you to question the expertise of the airline's quality control?

"Mind your own business" is an adage that carries weight outdoors. Rafters and other enthusiasts are a friendly but independent lot and rarely crave unsolicited advice. After all, solitude and privacy contribute to the outdoors' appeal. But what circumstances call for one to break that silence?

That question faced me, then 28, on the Stanislaus River in the stormy spring of 1978. A crack crew and I braved the Camp 9 to Parrott's Ferry run as the river pumped out enough water to put a football field 10 feet under in less than 30 seconds.

It had been snowing non-stop for over a week in the high country northwest of Yosemite, and now a deluge of rain was melting it away like butter in a hot frying pan. Boaters like us lived for such times, when the river reached its maximum level and we could test our skills and equipment to the limit while having the ride of our lives. However, this time around, a poorly prepared party created our greatest challenge.

I had assembled an ideal crew to match the demands of a trip riding the dragon's back of a river in flood. We were six veteran boaters in two self-bailing oar rigs called Huck Finns, designed and built by the legendary Bryce Whitmore in 1966. Huck Finns look like a giant air mattress with four tubes laced together, with one person rowing a pair of 10-foot oars from the stern, and two nimble souls near the bow jumping on the ever-changing high side of the boat to keep it from flipping. I captained one boat, and my longtime navigational partner, Chris Condon, led the other.

We were joined by fellow Sierra foothill residents Mike Nelson and Tom Cornett, both intrepid entrepreneurs and partners in crime on several eccentric whitewater expeditions. Like me, they had migrated from the northern California coast and had lots of experience surfing the big waves of the Pacific. Mark Dubois and Fred Dennis, early pioneers of the river conservation movement and highly skilled navigators in their own right, had come to gawk at the mesmerizing floodwaters and were easily enticed to join us.

This same veteran group in 1973 had made the first descent of the Cherry Creek/Upper Tuolumne run (now considered the most challenging commercial rafting run in the US) in self-bailing catarafts I designed and built for the task. I had been running high water trips on the Stan and the nearby Tuolumne for more than 13 years and was at the top of my game.

In spite of the pounding rain, we had an excellent run the first day. The river was flowing around 14,000 cfs, 12 times the normal summertime level. The shoreline, a lethal tangle of fallen trees, overhanging branches, and swift current, was to be avoided at all costs. But if you stayed out in middle on the writhing spine of the rampaging dragon, you could dance with her, and that we did. On the next day we came back for more.

The intensity of the storm increased. The rain was so thick that those of us with glasses couldn't see. The narrow seams in the cliffs above us, normally dry, gushed with torrential runoff and created dramatic waterfalls. The river had risen so fast that the parking lot was under nearly a foot of water. The Stan roared past us at 18,000 cfs. By the time we pushed off, it neared 23,000, and the river peaked that day at around 28,000 cfs.

But we were not the only boaters launching a trip that day. Another group of river guides prepared for an overnight excursion just behind us. Since we were at the higher end of the "acceptable level of risk" spectrum for whitewater boating on the Stan, I had a short chat with them while we were all rigging. They were professional guides, so I didn't say much, but I did tell them about our run the day before and departed with a "have fun."

As we were getting into our final take-off position, I noticed that their loads were inordinately large and unwieldy—too big for the task at hand. They even had a pile of folded lawn chairs (also known as death traps) strapped to the top. You could barely see the rowers' heads through their haystacks of gear. Even more troubling, none of them wore wetsuits, an absolute necessity on high water trips where getting catapulted into a frigid river is a very real possibility.

Breaking the eddy fence (or I should say a randomly oscillating 4-foot water wall) at the put-in to peel out was one of the biggest challenges of the day. From then on, the main driving force of the river looked pretty clean. As we flushed out into the main current, making a sharp U-turn downstream, I worried about the other boaters' fate. I looked over my shoulder to see them with their thumbs up, cheering us on through the gray curtain. I couldn't help but think that they would be in trouble very soon. But my focus turned to the task at hand: staying on line as we approached Death Rock.

Death Rock got its name in the late 1960s after a springtime outing went very wrong. A group of scouts had each made their own "rafts," glorified inner tubes with glued-in floors in which the boys sat cross legged, enveloped in rain ponchos, secured around their waists with rope and tied again to the bottom of the tubes.

The young boys took off from shore in the promising sunshine with no idea what they were up against. The water was cold and high. Few, if any, wore PFDs. Like a wayward school of guppies, the boys were quickly scattered in all directions, totally out of control. Fishermen dotting the shoreline hauled them out the best they could, but one was not so lucky. He drifted right into the hole at the then-unnamed Death Rock, immediately flipped over, and was caught in the backwash of the slurping maw. Bryce Whitmore, the first outfitter on the Stan, grabbed him just above Devil's Staircase, but by that time he was dead. The force of the hydraulics had turned the poncho into a ballooning sea anchor, pinching him off around the base of his spine so that his torso collapsed almost to the size of his backbone. The foolhardy adventure is well-known among river guides of the Stan.

As we approached Death Rock, we saw that it was now fully submerged. This created a huge sucking hole that could easily swallow several Winnebagos at once. The trees along the shoreline had major rapids flowing through them with a deadly thrashing of straining limbs and debris. Since we knew what to expect, we made the move early on to avoid the worst of it by paddling around the feature.

The first place we could safely stop was 3 miles downstream, just below the confluence with Rose Creek. With intuition born of many years on the river, Chris and I smelled trouble and decided to wait. I hovered on the eddy line, working it back and forth, up and down, in circles and angles, waiting. Chris pulled over to an open area on the shoreline, doing all he could to stay in one place. Within minutes, a few oars, an ice chest, and other flotsam came floating by, including a lifeless lump of humanity with only the top of his head barely visible.

I peeled out into the current making chase to intercept the body as it drifted toward the ugly strainers above Mother Rapid. If he wasn't already dead, they would certainly do him in, locking him in their lethal web and keeping his head underwater for good. In desperate voices we yelled at the body to "Swim right, swim right!" Miraculously, his arms actually started flopping in the correct direction, and he narrowly missed an ugly fate.

He was in the main current now and immediately picked up speed as he entered the freight train of standing waves below. It would be extremely difficult for even the most seasoned of guides to survive a swim like this, especially after all he had been through already. I was doing all I could to catch him, rowing backwards through the thunderous wave train at full speed, deflecting the current to my advantage and trying to stay on line so that we wouldn't become victims of high water ourselves. Hot pursuit of a body in a whitewater river requires perfect timing and exceptional navigation. Bodies are like submarines, plowing through rapids at a surprisingly fast clip. Rafts are slower, subject to the various currents, waves and other river features that hinder speedy downstream progress. Walls of water kept pushing us back upstream and slowed our pursuit. He was still out in front, headed full steam toward Razor Back. Finally, we caught up to him just above the entry turn and hauled his nearly lifeless body aboard as I swung into shore. The guy wasn't wearing a wetsuit and suffered from hypothermia. He vomited and passed out.

After a while he came round and told us of his epic. Within the first five minutes he had flipped in the hole at Death Rock, and like a good river guide, crawled onto the top of his overturned raft to assist the rescue of his own craft. Unfortunately the rescue didn't come, and he was carried by the merciless river on his upside-down raft into the powerful laterals at the Rose Creek confluence, where he flipped a second time.

We stabilized his condition and tended to his other wounds the best we could. A few very wet and cold hours later, his group finally caught up to us, shaken up from their own dramas but all intact and very happy to see him standing on the shore with us. Most of their crew hiked out from there. Those who remained followed our boats to the takeout at Parrott's Ferry, which we almost missed due to thick fog that settled into the canyon.

I don't remember his name, but every once in a while we meet at a Friends of the River conference or on the banks of the Tuolumne. Each time, he makes a point of giving me a hug and a big smile of thanks, reminding me that I saved his life. It's an interesting energy exchange that makes me slightly uncomfortable, as I only did what comes naturally to most people who spend their lives with rivers. I do know that I used every bit of my expertise during that rescue which marked a peak in the arc of my performance and the culmination of years of experience running high water trips. We had the right crew, the right equipment, and the right blend of strength, skill, foresight, and chutzpah required to make a successful interception and dance with the dragon.

Forty-five years of river running has taught me that in any given rapid, even the shortest distance must be navigated with wisdom and respect, and there is no substitute for the long and bumpy road of experience . . . and I wouldn't get on that plane!

A whitewater legend, a seasoned guide, and founder of Sierra Mac River Trips, Marty McDonnell is known far and wide as a pioneer of California whitewater. His river running designs for rafts were revolutionary and allowed many "unrunnable" sections of river to be explored and enjoyed by thousands of river enthusiasts. ■

CHAPTER 12

TYING KNOTS LIKE A PRO

Proficiency in Knot Tying

Knot tying is an essential skill set for the river rescue technician. The reality is that not all rescuers will become comfortable or competent swimming through rapids, throwing ropes, or wading in challenging terrain. All rescuers should, however, be competent at tying all of the knots and hitches introduced in this chapter. Tying knots takes practice. Nurture a culture that doesn't accept comments such as, "I'm terrible at knots." Instead, encourage all team members to make the time to regularly practice knot tying until they are proficient.

It is important that rescuers be able to tie these knots on the spot in a minute or less. Each attempt should be smooth and flawless and result in a

How solid is that knot? A belay is only as good as its connection to the swimmer.

knot that is dressed, set, and has adequate tail. The emotions and distractions of a rescue can be overwhelming. Practice tying knots with cold, wet hands and also with gloves on. Practice tying knots blindfolded or with your hands underwater. Do what you can to become a knot ninja.

TERMINOLOGY

Knot. A tied portion of rope, cord, or webbing using just the rope, cord, or webbing itself.

Hitch. A portion of rope or webbing tied around another object.

Bend. A combination of knots to connect two ends of rope or webbing.

Loop. A piece of rope that is crossed.

Bight. A pinch of rope.

Standing end. The inactive end of the rope.

Running or working end. The active end of the rope that is used to tie the knot.

Tail. Excess rope after a knot, hitch, or bend has been tied. Typically the tail should be about 4 to 6 inches long.

Understanding knot terminology and anatomy makes rescuers better instructors for others on their team. A *bight* is created when a U in the rope is formed. Once the rope crosses over, it becomes a *loop*. If the running end of your loop is on top of the rope as you look at it, then it's an overhand loop. These reference terms can be useful when teaching others about knots.

BIGHT   LOOP

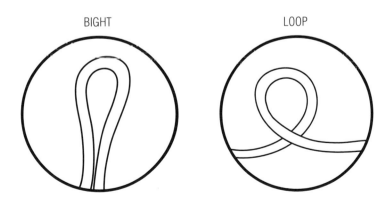

are both "friction hitches" that slide when slack but bind and hold under load. Use the prusik when working with rope, and the klemheist for webbing.

COILS
Two different styles for throwing coils or string rope: the butterfly coil and the mountaineer's coil.

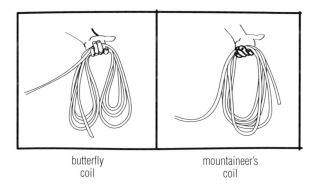

butterfly
coil

mountaineer's
coil

CHAPTER 13

BOAT-BASED RESCUES AND RECOVERIES

Rescuing Swimmers and Recovering Gear from Rafts, Canoes, and Kayaks

Boats can serve as effective rescue platforms. They can access points in the river that would otherwise be unreachable and can be used to conduct searches and chases much faster than a rescuer walking along the riverbank can manage. In rescue situations, boats must be navigated by competent rescuers with considerable whitewater experience. Just because you own a tool doesn't mean you're qualified to use it. Seek out professional instruction on

Rescuers practice boat maneuvering with a Hyside Paddle Cat in the Class V Cribworks Rapid on the on the West Branch of the Penobscot River, Maine. Accessing or transporting your patient may require solid boat skills. SACHA JACKSON

■ A RIVER NARRATIVE: INITIATION ENTRAPMENT

By Nate Ostis

In September 1999, a woman almost drowned in Initiation Rapid on the upper Gauley River in West Virginia. Initiation Rapid is only Class III and just a few hundred yards downstream from the put-in, but it is one of the deadliest sections of the 26-mile run. A huge boulder sieve lurks in the middle of the river, hidden by a very inviting series of 6-foot waves. Over the years, several paddlers have been killed here.

If run properly, however, one can negotiate the waves and slip right down beside the sieve and actually look into its deep nastiness. I was shooting video for a commercial raft company that autumn, and gazing into the maw of Initiation Rapid as I passed had become sort of a routine for me as I paddled by every day. One foggy morning, though, when I glanced down, I saw a sixty-year-old woman, with only her head exposed, screaming for her life.

Apparently, she had fallen out of a commercial raft from another company ahead of our trip and slipped into one of the cracks of the sieve. She was oriented facing upstream with her legs stuck in the rock up to her knees. Her hands were grasping the crack on either side of her knees, preventing the oncoming water from pushing her onto her back and thus becoming submerged. Because she was located in the middle of the river, her guides on shore were unable to offer her any assistance, but they were signaling for help. I quickly caught the small eddy below the sieve and took stock of the situation. If she were to lose her grip, the force of the current would hold her down. She would not be savable. I yelled to her to hold on with everything she had and that I was on my way.

I had my work cut out for me. The top of the rock was 4 feet above water level, which made it awkward to get out of my boat. It took me about two minutes just to climb out, balance myself standing on the seat, clamber onto the rock, and then raise my boat out of the water and set it on the rock. Once there, I could see her—8 feet away from me and crying hysterically that she was going to die and all she wanted was her grandchildren.

It was a stressful situation. I needed to get to her fast, but I had to make sure I didn't either fall in one of the cracks or slip into the downstream current and get washed away. The terrain between myself and the woman was a 45-degree slope of solid rock with a foot of strong current rushing over. I slowly traversed over to her on an underwater micro-ledge, and about a minute later I was within two feet. I clearly remember her shrieking, "I can't hold on anymore, I'm gonna die."

I started thinking about possible outcomes, and of me living the rest of my life thinking, "I was so close, and then she just slipped away."

I managed to step across her so one foot was positioned on either side of the crack she was stuck in. I reached down and grabbed her by the lapels of her PFD and lifted her straight into the air so we were face to face. She likely weighed around 120 pounds, but my adrenaline made her feel like 30 pounds. Although she was now free, I had raised our collective center of gravity too high to remain balanced for very long. "We have to jump!" I yelled and off we went into the downstream run-out below. I held onto her the entire way, and as we surfaced, we received a throw rope from one of her trip's rafts and were pulled to safety.

In the aftermath I found myself overwhelmed with emotions. I had never been put to the test like that before. I had no one to consult and no time to think. *Save the woman.* That was all I knew at that point; everything else just had to work. Things could have easily gone very differently for both of us. We were lucky. This was instrumental in my paddling career. From that point on, I decided to relentlessly study swiftwater rescue and wilderness first aid. I decided being proactive is way more rewarding than simply relying on ill-prepared, poorly practiced, reactive decision-making. I've been a dedicated student of rescue and first aid ever since.

Nate Ostis is the author of the NOLS River Rescue Guide *and an editor of the* NOLS River Educator Notebook. *He is a senior field instructor for NOLS and the founder of Wilderness Rescue International.* ◼

CHAPTER 14

ENTRAPMENT RESCUES AND RECOVERIES

Managing Foot, Body, and Boat Entrapments

An entrapment is one of the scariest and most challenging scenarios a rescuer can face. The amount of time we have to rescue an entrapped patient is potentially quite short. Successful rescues are often the result of good luck and efficient, highly skilled rescuers with the ability to adapt to their environment. Over the years, rescuers have experimented with many different solutions for entrapments. Explore as many solutions as you can in a controlled practice environment, and decide which techniques are

Heads-down patients are those whose airway has been submersed or who are positioned such that rescuers cannot be sure of their ability to breath.

worth considering in the future for your team. The solutions in this chapter were chosen for their simplicity and probability of success. Entrapment is a significant concern in every rescue response and teams need to have pre-planned their systems prior to needing them in a real event.

TYPES OF ENTRAPMENT

- **Foot entrapment.** The patient's foot is stuck on the bottom of the river, and the force of the current prevents her from freeing herself.
- **Body entrapment.** The patient's body is stuck in an undercut rock, strainer, crack, pothole, or in between rocks.
- **Boat entrapment.** The patient is stuck inside her craft while pinned against a rock or is trapped in between her boat and a rock.

A foot entrapment is a serious, life-threatening situation. Prevention is critical and pre-planned responses are a must.

PRINCIPLES OF ENTRAPMENT RESCUES

Resources. The right number of rescuers is the minimum required to do the job effectively. There are often several possible solutions, and there's room for innovation and creativity. Prepare additional rescuers to not overwhelm a rescue scene with their presence but to anticipate they may be called upon as needed. Appreciate the need for both directive leadership and active followership. (For more on leadership, see page 241.)

Spotters. Establish upstream spotters to look for boat traffic and debris. Downstream spotters ideally include both throw bag rescuers and a tethered rescue swimmer on belay. An entrapped patient has the potential of becoming an unresponsive swimmer heading downstream. Be ready.

Contingency planning. Create multiple plans of attack, and don't be surprised if they don't work. Have a Plan A, Plan B, Plan C, and so on. Be ready for several attempts at various ideas. Be flexible and open-minded as

to try to reverse the entrapment. This technique can be quickly referred to as *pull to pop*. Coach the patient on what you are doing, and ask her to tell you if it is making the situation worse or causing any significant pain.

Heads-Up Patients: One-Shore-Based Rescue

When the patient is within approximately 30 feet of shore, there are some one-shore-based options. These may be considered even when a two-shore-based approach could work but your time or resources are limited.

THROW AND RETRIEVE

Throw a 70-foot throw bag with the goal of hitting the water a few feet upstream of the patient. The current will carry the rope downstream to the patient, and the excess will continue on downstream directly below the patient. The end of the rope that is now in the water must be retrieved back to shore. You have some options for doing this. Namely, either wade to retrieve the line, hook it with a stick or paddle, or use a snag plate attached to a second throw bag.

SNAG PLATE

If available, use a throw bag retrofitted with a snag plate. Deploy the bag fully on the ground in front of you, so the installed snag plate is exposed. Place a baseball-size rock into the empty throw bag, and cinch it shut with the draw string. Pinch the rope just above the snag plate using your middle and ring fingers, and butterfly coil the rope. Throw the rope beyond the line in the river, and then pull it back in to snag the throw bag in the water.

LOOP TOSS

Deploy the throw bag fully on the ground. Have one rescuer grab one end of the rope and another rescuer grab the opposite end. Both rescuers begin butterfly coiling toward the center of the rope. Once both rescuers have fully coiled the rope into their hands, they are ready to throw a loop or bight of rope out over the patient.

After the rope is thrown, the loop of rope is now over the patient with both ends on shore. The downstream rescuer now moves upstream and underneath the rope of the other rescuer. They continue upstream as far as the rope will allow to get the best angle of pull. This line now serves as the stabilization line, and the downstream rescuer serves as the cinch line. Ask the patient if she is now able to free herself. Consider the possibility of boating, wading, or swimming out to the patient. If none of these options will work, consider doing a coordinated pull to pop to try and release the entrapment.

One-shore-based rescue. Pause at the height of your backswing to keep the rope coils from tangling.

Follow through, pointing at your target or just slightly above it.

A smooth and firm toss is better than a fast and jerky one.

The downstream rescuer now walks upstream and travels underneath the other belayer's line. This creates the cinch.

Heads-Down Patient

A heads-down entrapment is a life or death matter. The imminent risk of death justifies extreme measures, even though they will probably cause injury. Try swimming directly for the patient and grab on to her body as you swim over her. Use the patient to stop your downstream progress, and then try to stand downstream of her. It's reasonable to tie a rope to a patient's arm or leg while trying to pull her free. Try to pull a person out of the entrapment the same way she went in; i.e., pull from upstream rather than pulling with the current. Because this patient has no airway, consider giving rescue breaths underwater to get oxygen to her immediately. If boating, wading, or swimming out to your patient does not work, consider the following rope system:

- Establish a line across the river on the downstream side of the patient with belayers on either end. This will work in distances less than 65 feet.
- Position two additional rescuers as solo waders in the water on either side. They will perform a one-person line astern wade using a paddle or 6-foot stick. On one end of the paddle or stick, affix a prusik cord with a clove hitch, and then tie the tails with an overhand to create a clippable shelf. Clip a carabiner through this shelf and onto the fixed line going across the river.

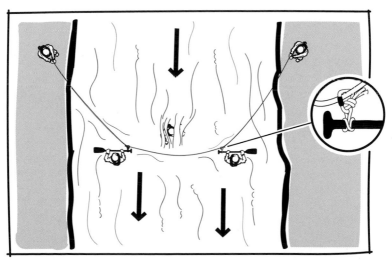

When dealing with a submerged, entrapped patient, rescuers can wade out and submerge the stabilization line while haul teams stationed upstream can pull the rope into position against the patient's torso. Once positioned, a further pull will hopefully bring the patient's head above water.

NOLS Instructors training in a head-down entrapment scenario. The yellow drybag anchored in the middle of the river simulates the entrapped patient.

- The wading rescuers advance their traverse to get as close to the patient as they can while still maintaining adequate control. The rope is held out of the water during this step.
- With the wading rescuers just downstream of the patient and the line, and as close to one another as possible, the belayers move upstream to create a 90-degree bend in the rope.
- Submerge the rope in a coordinated effort and watch it in the water. Manipulate the rope to get it around the submerged patient's torso. This could also be done by hand if paddles, prusiks, and carabiners were not readily available. Signal to the belayers to take up rope while continuing to manipulate the line with the paddles.
- With skill and good luck, the rope should bring the patient's torso up and out of the water. Wading rescuers might have to let go of the attached paddles during this process and either swim or wade back to shore.
- With the patient's torso now above water, consider applying the two-line cinch (aka the Super Cinch) to secure her more completely. This allows the extrication line to pull with greater confidence that patient contact will not be lost. This arrangement has the potential of putting a tremendous amount of force on the patient's thoracic cavity and therefore should only be used in extreme rescue situations or obvious recovery scenarios, such as a heads down patient missing for days.

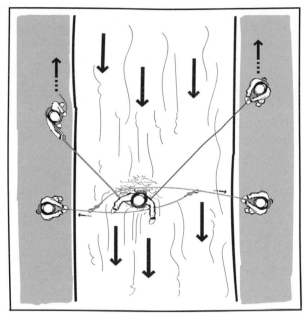

The Super Cinch. Upstream rescuer tosses throw bag across the river. Opposite shore tosses a second throw bag back across the river on the downstream side of the patient. The ends of the throw bag get clipped to the opposite lines with carabiners to create a quick and aggressive cinching system.

Limited-Slip Girth Hitch

This is an advanced specialty hitch designed to secure a patient by the wrist without damaging tissue. This is an accepted solution for stabilizing a patient trapped in an under-cut rock or strainer. It is intended for stabilization and not necessarily extraction. Do not pull with so much force that the patient's shoulder pops out, but rather apply enough pressure to support her breathing. Remember to go back to the ABCs of basic first aid. Without an airway, we have no patient, so stabilizing breathing is the first priority. We achieve this by pulling with enough force to keep her head, and therefore her airway, above water.

The limited-slip girth hitch is simply a girth hitch on top of another girth hitch, which reduces the amount it can cinch. If possible, use webbing for this hitch since it cuts into the skin less than rope, but in the heat of the moment either will do fine. When seconds count, use a regular girth hitch or any other knot that will work in order to keep the patient's airway open. This knot is especially useful in this situation because it limits the

A simulated undercut scenario, showing the use of a limited-slip girth hitch around the patient's wrist to stabilize the airway.

pain and permanent tissue damage that will take place if it is left in place for an extended period. A patient in less pain means less screaming, more energy reserves, and more effective communication.

To be prepared for such an event, consider having a rescue belt made of webbing, tied in a loop, and double wrapped around the waist. This can double as an anchor piece, and as a flip-line for paddle rafts.

To tie the limited-slip girth hitch, grab the line with both hands, then make two consecutive loops in each hand and in opposing directions. Put the two resulting loops together, and slip over patient's hand.

■ A RIVER NARRATIVE: HIGH WATER MOOSE

By John Connelly

Rapid-pool rivers should lend themselves to running organized, well-paced raft trips, with ample recovery zones below hard rapids. But on the lower Moose River in the Adirondack Mountains of upstate New York, the combination of spring floods and ice-laden water really ups the ante.

It's a short spring season that can see flows from, "How low can you go?" to, "If z boat doesn't flip, it'll be a miracle." It's not for everyone—guides as well as paying customers.

The increased speed, enlarged water features, and the shortening or complete disappearance of recovery zones between rapids increase both the rapids' difficulty and the consequences, making it a very different risk management challenge for trip leaders, raft guides and safety boaters. The Moose is not your average raft trip.

This particular day was not to be your average raft trip either. Our company had approximately sixty paying customers in wetsuits arrive in buses and trudge through calf-deep snow toward the put-in. We had eight rafts floating in fast whitewater with guides standing by. The swollen river flashed behind them with the occasional table-size chunk of ice tumbling by.

As bizarre as it all sounds, these were typical early season high water, spring run-off raft trips and exactly what everyone had signed up to do, including the guides. Early season attracted true adventurers, but also some of the not-quite-right clientele that wanted everything extreme and for whom "safe" was a four-letter-word. If they didn't go for a swim, flip the raft, or otherwise nearly meet their maker, guides stood a chance of getting stiffed with no tip at day's end.

The trip began, and away we went. We had the usual swimmers in major rapids, with throw bags flying through the air and customers being hauled back aboard like tuna on a gaff. There had been no outright flips, but then our situation changed drastically.

I was the trip leader in the lead raft. I was responsible for running rapids first and setting up safety, in the form of readying my crew to become a chase boat if needed and being the rescue rope provider at the bottom of major rapids. I could also direct traffic, stopping the next raft in the queue if there was an issue and sending the next raft when all was clear. Needless to say, my runs had to be clean and uneventful, as there was no one available to clean up my mess, should I have one.

Froth Hole was a notorious rapid. The contours converge, and there it is, Froth Hole, a 10- to 12-foot river-wide ledge dropping into a huge recirculating hole. One by one, the raft guides checked-off that it was clear to go and peeled out of the holding eddy and ran the drop—with varying degrees of grace, but all clean.

One of the last rafts to come down was a little left of the ideal approach line. Over the center of the ledge into the maw of Froth Hole they went. Sixteen feet of raft with seven paddlers and their guide was gone from sight. In an instant they surfaced, firmly stuck in the churning recycling whitewater. The raft began to spin as it filled with water and surfed back into the hole again and again. One by one, paddlers flew out of the spinning, bucking raft that now resembled a rodeo ride at a cowboy bar. The guide tried to stop the spinning with her paddle, but it was futile. The raft kept spinning and bodies kept flying until the only one remaining was the guide. The swimming passengers were hauled into shore with various throw bag tosses.

I lined up the soggy passengers we had just rescued, and impressed them into service. We threw the guide in the recirculating raft a throw bag and had everyone pull. It took only a moment to free the raft from the grips of the hole and pendulum-swing into shore below my group. But in the middle of all this, something bad happened.

When we pulled on the rope, the guy in front of me fell to the ground, holding his neck and not moving. "I felt something go in my neck." he said. I immediately grabbed his head to protect his spine. Our company placed backboards at all major rapids that we had operations on. We packaged the patient on a readily-available backboard and began the carry out. All the guides and clients took turns with the carry. It was about a mile out of the river canyon in knee-deep snow. The ambulance was waiting when we got to the road with our patient, and off they went to the nearest hospital.

The patient ended up having a fractured third cervical vertebra in his neck. He was admitted at a specialized facility complete with a wire halo screwed into his skull to prevent movement for the following six months. He was thankful for the professional care he had received from our company and stated he knew the risks of rafting dangerous whitewater. No blame was directed in the incident as we reconstructed the events to determine how he sustained the injury.

The patient had been violently ejected while the raft was surfing and surging about in the hole. As if on a springboard, he catapulted across the raft and actually penetrated the curtain of falling water. He apparently struck the ledge that made the drop, hitting it under the bottom of the back of his helmet and above the collar of his lifejacket. Bingo . . . cervical vertebra number three.

My takeaways from this incident are as follows: First, there are good people in the world. Our injured guest recognized and accepted the inherent risks of the activity. He chose the activity and these specific conditions because of the challenge, adventure, and yes, potential consequences. Furthermore, under pressure from the media to indict our guide and our company, he took the moral high-ground and spoke the truth. The guide felt terrible about the injury sustained, but she performed like a true professional and recognized that these things do happen in adventure activities. We stayed in touch with our client throughout the following years as we cared deeply for his well-being.

Also, we invested in incremental training at high water levels so that our guides were accustomed to running the river at those levels and were proficient. Outfitters that trained on lower water and ran trips on high water frequently produced spectacularly bad results. Disaster simulations and scenarios during guide training really paid off. Having a public relations and risk management plan in place to manage communications with first responders, medical staff, friends and family of an injured guest, and the media proved to be vitally important.

John Connelly founded Eastern River Expeditions, running whitewater trips throughout the Eastern United States. He served as president of the Eastern Professional River Outfitters Association, was a founding board member of the America Outdoors Association, and served as a risk manager and incident investigator for the Worldwide Outfitters and Guides Association. ■

Spread calm. Dissect your mistakes after the situation has been dealt with.

CHAPTER 15

PINNED BOATS AND EXTRICATIONS

Anatomy of a Pin

A pinned boat is one that has become entrapped or stuck on the riverbed or man-made structures and is held in this position by the oncoming current. Rocks, trees, fences, dams, and bridges are all common causes of pinned boats. The other primary causes of pinned boats are human error, poor judgment and decision-making, and mistaken boat navigation. Managing a scene with a boat pinned in the middle of a rapid can take hours or days to resolve, particularly if rescuers on scene are unfamiliar with the strategies necessary to recover the craft. Quiz your team on a regular basis to be sure the content of this chapter is well understood and practiced.

Rescuers should be familiar with the general ways in which a boat is pinned or stuck on rocks and other obstructions. By becoming familiar with the arrangement of particular pins, we can be far more efficient in their extrications. Have a solid understanding of what the following terms mean: center pin, end-to-end pin, pinch pin, vertical pin, and flat pin.

Center pin. This pin occurs when a boat is swept sideways onto a rock or obstruction. The force of current on the boat results in the bow and stern wrapping around the rock.

End-to-end pin. This pin is a result of the bow and stern of the boat each getting stuck on different rocks. The boat then collapses in the center where there is the most force and least support.

Vertical pin. When a boat goes over a steep but shallow ledge system, the bow can dive under and become wedged on the riverbed floor. The paddler can easily become entrapped by the force of the water. This usually occurs with canoes or kayaks and less frequently with rafts, and can lead to a pitch-pole pin.

CHAPTER 17

MECHANICAL ADVANTAGE SYSTEMS

Rescuers need to be able to build a proper rope system anchor and set up a mechanical advantage system in a quick and efficient manner without the supervision of another rescuer. Ideally, team members will be available to double-check one another, but in reality we must not be dependent on fellow rescuers.

Key Principles for Mechanical Advantage Systems

Units of force = number of pullers x mechanical advantage

For example, if you have ten people pulling on a 3:1, you will have 30 units of force. Most adults can pull 50 percent of their body weight, or more. These are some key principles for you to keep in mind:

Hauling as a team takes practice to do efficiently.

Evaluate. Completely evaluate the scene to assess river hazards such as river currents, rapids, obstacles, and accessibility to the boat and anchor possibilities. Go slow to go fast. Anticipate the variables that are required to perform a successful extraction.

Lead. When possible, designate a hands-off leader or incident coordinator (IC) that supervises the big picture operation and overall risk management. Deploy upstream spotters to look for debris floating downstream and to notify any upstream boat traffic that an incident is occurring. Downstream spotters should also be deployed, and be ready to secure a runaway boat or a rescuer that slips and becomes unresponsive in the water.

Protect. All persons involved with the extrication and within 10 feet of shore need to wear helmets and PFDs. This helps with both the unexpected swim as well as tripping or falling into rocks should the mechanical advantage system break or fail. Rescuers need to have knives readily available for emergency use with ropes. Closed-toe shoes are more effective than open-toe sandals in preventing foot injuries.

Plan. Create a detailed plan, and be sure to articulate expectations for roles and communications. Mechanical advantage is often considered in recovery situations where time is not a pressing issue. Generate multiple plans of attack, and be flexible with your approach. Often several strategies need to be experimented with before you discover the solution that produces the desired outcome. Clarify as needed to be sure everyone understands their roles and the signals to be used prior to generating mechanical forces. Identify specific potential failure points. Verify that no persons are at risk of being struck by elements of flying or broken gear under pressure. Ask yourself: *If this system does fail, how will that affect the rescuers pulling on the rope? Will they topple over into sharp rocks or over an embankment?*

Construct. Building mechanical advantage is similar to building a homemade shotgun. Mechanical advantage systems have the potential of failing under tremendous force, resulting in heavy gear flying through the air and hurting people. Recovering gear is our fifth priority as a rescuer and team members should not be exposed to unnecessary risk when extricating boats that are stuck in the river.

Pulleys are preferred over carabiners for change of direction due to friction. Anchors need to be solid prior to loading. Ask another teammate to check your work and look for possible improvements. Hundreds or thousands of pounds of force will be loaded on this system. Take your time, and be efficient. Remember: Simple is good. The more complex the system, the more components that can potentially fail.

Systems greater than 12:1 begin to reach a point of diminishing returns due to friction and complexity. Additionally, a system greater than 12:1 drastically increases the potential failure points.

The Redirecting Pulley is a Critical Consideration

The consequences of catastrophic equipment failure can be minimized if personnel are not at risk of being injured. This is achieved with the redirecting pulley. All haul systems, even a simple 1:1, should ideally be built with a redirecting pulley off a shore-based anchor. Properly set redirecting pulleys dramatically reduce the potential for injury should the entire system fail and send hard gear flying in the air. Mechanical advantage systems have the potential of generating thousands of pounds of force, and if components fail under this load, then gear can shoot through the air like bullets and cause serious injury to personnel on scene. Some mechanical advantage is lost when using a redirecting pulley but reducing the risk of injury can be worth any diminished results. If you choose not to install a redirecting pulley, then you must be certain no people are at risk of getting hit by flying components should the system fail.

Redirect pulleys are not a new concept. For decades these pulleys were proposed as an environmental consideration when haul teams were unable to pull directly in toward shore due to a cliff wall, boulder field, or thick grove of vegetation. Now we are setting a new standard, stating that these critical pulleys should be considered for all systems and only discarded after the rescue team agrees that no personnel are at risk of injury during the hauling sequence.

Redirects are also referred to as change of direction pulleys or CODs. Carabiners make poor pulleys, as they create too much friction. Plan ahead so you have the appropriate number of pulleys. If you anticipate building a 3:1 system, you need to carry three pulleys. A simple 5:1 or compound 9:1 system requires five pulleys.

Redirects must change the direction of pull by 90 degrees to keep haulers out of the line of fire should the anchor fail and fly outward. In addition, no one should stand inside the angle, to further reduce the risk. The re-directing pulley does result in some loss of mechanical advantage efficiency, but the advantage of minimizing rescuer injury should be valued more.

Additional Safety Features

Dampeners. Secure a buoyant object (such as an extra PFD or empty 5-gallon jug) to any haul line that has the potential to break and fly back toward rescuers. Clip it directly to a prusik, and slide it as close to the likely breaking point as possible. By using a buoyant object, the gear in play should not fly as far, should stay afloat, and should not create new entrapment hazards if the system breaks. Dampeners should not be viewed as

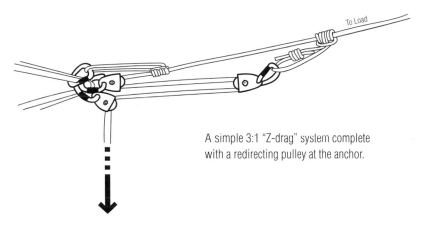

A simple 3:1 "Z-drag" system complete with a redirecting pulley at the anchor.

adequate substitution of a redirecting pulley, however. Rescuers should not be at risk of being hit by anything, even a PFD rapidly flying toward them.

Prusik hitch cordelettes. The cordelette you choose for your system should be of high tensile strength and of the appropriate diameter in relation to the haul line; too big, and a friction hitch won't grip the haul line. Cordelette should be approximately two-thirds the thickness of the haul line. For example, if your haul line is 9 millimeters, you should apply a prusik hitch with 6-millimeter cordelette. However, don't go too small; cordelettes get weaker as they get thinner. Typical cordelettes will measure 6 to 8 millimeters.

Anticipate that prusiks are the weak link in the system and are what will likely break first (depending on your attachment points on the craft).

Store prusik hitch cordelettes loosely knotted or unknotted and out of direct sunlight.

some time to marinate in your group's collective mind before moving on. Don't be in a rush to haul before adequate re-assessment has occurred.

2. "Anybody *not* ready to haul?" If the team is ready, they just stand by quietly with eyes on the team leader to indicate understanding.

3. "OK. Haul on three. One, two, three, haul!" Continue with counted hauls on a three-count until your boat has been extricated or you're ready for a break.

4. "Stop and Hold! One, two, three, four, five." After making your last pull as a team and before running blindly back into the Danger Zone, first give the system an extra window of time to fail if necessary. Give the system a clock count of five seconds after the last haul before running in to set the brake.

5. "Set the brake!" Sometimes the brake prusik will set itself into the locking position without any necessary assistance from team members. Other times a team member in full river rescue personal protective equipment will need to enter into the danger zone to set the brake manually. Immediately vacate the danger zone after setting the brake and avoid the temptation to linger or loiter in this very unsafe location.

6. "Reset the system!" After setting the brake, and prior to hauling again, it often will make sense to reset the system. Extend the pulley prusiks out as far as possible prior to hauling again. This should not be done casually. Remember the system is fully loaded and the longer you stay in this dangerous area, the longer you are exposed to potential injury.

CHAPTER 18

SPECIAL CONSIDERATIONS

Rope Ferries

Ferrying a rope across the river can assist in several operations discussed throughout this book, including Telfer lowers, tensioned diagonals, stabilizing and extrication lines for foot entrapment, and wading assist lines. On many rivers the distance between riverbanks is too great for this skill to be of much use. However, there are rapids, constrictions, midstream eddies, and channels created by islands where ferrying a line can be very effective to establish a rope across the current. The other option for establishing a rope across the channel would be to make a throw bag toss (or use a launcher) between two rescuers standing on opposite sides of the channel.

Dealing with unusual situations means adapting to your environment and thinking outside the box. TOBY HAWKINS

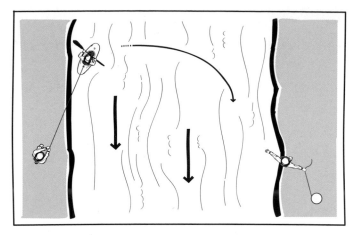

A kayak (or other boat) can ferry a rope across a river too wide for a throw. Launch well upstream from the intended target on the far bank. The belayer should hold just enough tension to keep the line from becoming entangled; don't hinder the kayaker's progress by hauling too hard, and be ready to give slack if needed.

A kayak or canoe is typically the fastest, most efficient way to ferry a rope. The next boat for consideration should be a paddle raft. If none of these are available, then a wading team or a swimmer may have to take the rope across. In a head-down situation, there may not be time to retrieve a boat for a rope ferry. Choose narrow channels to practice this skill, or target a midstream eddy as your destination.

The surface area of a $\frac{3}{8}$-inch rope extending 60 feet across the river is about 2 square feet. This can cause considerable drag, and every effort should be made to limit this drag prior to the attempt. Take the extra time to make the first attempt successful. Discuss what the person on shore can do to eliminate drag (hold it up high, skip it upstream, feed out adequate slack). Explain the benefits of using the current to your advantage by having the ferrying boat start upstream of the person holding the line to create a pendulum effect to the target area on the opposing shore. Emphasize speed and finesse.

When possible, have another rescuer waiting on the opposite shore to grab the line from the ferrying craft or swimmer. It can be very difficult for the ferrying paddler/swimmer to get out of the water while connected to the line.

The most ideal way to carry a rope is on a rescue PFD with a releasable harness. Holding it with one hand in a releasable grip is another option. Avoid using your teeth, as considerable damage can occur to teeth, gums, mouth, and face when the line goes taut. Do not tie it or wrap it around any part of your body.

Understand the benefits and disadvantages of using a messenger line. A messenger line is a long, thin, strong piece of string such as parachute cord. Having less weight and surface area, it is easier to pull across the river. A stronger rope is attached to the end and pulled across after. However, messenger lines can be very fussy to deal with. They often turn into a pile of tangled spaghetti when you are attempting to pay them out. When seconds count, it is sometimes better to just use a heavy line and take every precaution to make the first attempt successful.

Recognize and realize some of the biggest concerns when ferrying a line:

- Ease of release: Can I let go of this rope if I need to? Will it get caught up and create another hazard if I do?
- Obstructions: Is it likely that the rope will get snagged on something while ferrying it across?
- Missing your route: What do I do if it takes longer than I anticipate to get the rope across, and I end up downstream? What is Plan B? What is Plan C?

Tensioned Diagonals or Zip Lines

Imagine that a raft is pinned in the middle of a challenging rapid and the sun is setting. Efforts to extricate the boat have been unsuccessful to this

Zip lines can be an effective rescue method. Ensure that the tether is easily releasable.

assisted rescue to escape. Rescuers must be incredibly careful to not become an additional patient on scene.

There are several options out there for consideration when it comes to rescuing a patient from a low-head dam. The most reasonable and least risky options require several trained and equipped personnel as well as readily available equipment and boats.

LINE ACROSS THE RIVER TECHNIQUE

Establish a stabilization line across the river using a long haul rope or multiple throw bags connected together. Set this up such that the patient cannot grab the line until both belay teams are ready, so that rescuers do not get pulled in unexpectedly. Introduce the stabilization line to the patient, have her hold on tight, then walk downstream to pull her free of the recirculation. A rescue swimmer can be tethered with two different ropes attached to her rescue PFD and then belayed into position to grab the patient if she's gone unresponsive.

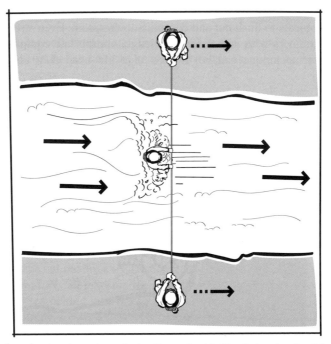

Timing a throw bag toss to reach a patient getting recirculated in a hole or low-head dam can be challenging. Another option is to extend a line to them intentionally using practiced belay teams on either shore. A responsive patient can grab the line and get pulled free from the hole as the rescuers on both banks walk downstream.

FOUR LINE BOAT RESCUE

A raft can serve as a great rescue platform when dealing with low-head dam scenarios. Attach a different rope to each corner of the boat and have four independent belayers work in harmony to position the boat to the patient. This technique can be done with only two ropes (on the upstream corners), but four lines give greater control of the boat and is the preferred method when resources allow.

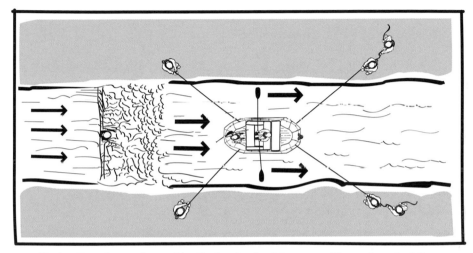

The four line raft rescue is a useful option in a low-head dam rescue. When well practiced, it can provide an intentional approach to a patient that is stuck in the powerful recirculation of the hydraulic.

Vehicles in the River

Managing vehicles in the river is something both river runners and professional rescuers should be prepared for. Getting to and from the river is often the most dangerous aspect of boating, and it often means traveling right along the river. Every second counts when vehicles enter the water, and having a good preplan in place could make the difference between a successful rescue and a tragic recovery.

Vehicles often end up in the river when drivers approach water over the road and attempt to cross the water anyways. As little as one or two feet of water can sweep a vehicle away. Many variables affect the behavior of a vehicle in the river, including speed of the current, position of the car in the river, and the design features of the car. Lower clearance lightweight vehicles will move easier than high clearance heavy vehicles. If the car is broadside to the current, then more force is acting on it, and it will move sooner than one that is in line with the current. Broadside vehicles are also very susceptible to rolling downstream, making it especially important for occupants and rescuers to consider concentrating their weight on the upstream side of the vehicle to keep it from rolling.

The composition of the riverbed bottom also greatly affects car behavior. Concrete and pavement in flooded streets or canals make it easier for the vehicle to slip along. Sand and gravel tend to help secure the vehicles from wanting to move since the water excavates the material under the tires, so the chassis rests on the riverbed. Muddy bottoms often sink the front of the car where the heavy engine is located.

Stabilize the vehicle before committing to extrication, so it does not float away or roll during the rescue attempt. If possible, tie off the vehicle to both riverbanks, since the vehicle will be more likely to shift as passenger weight is removed. Have PFDs available for the vehicle's occupants. Once the vehicle is stabilized, rescuers can begin their approach using reasonable and prudent techniques within their acceptable level of risk. Use the eddy created by the vehicle as the access point for swimming, wading, or boating. Do not approach from the upstream side, since the vehicle is acting as

A vehicle in the river creates a unique hazard that is unstable, potentially mobile, and full of entrapment potential. TOBY HAWKINS

NOLS Wilderness Medicine and Rescue Semester students train here in high-angle rope rescue techniques. EVAN HORN

an undercut rock or strainer. Having a readily available window punch could be very helpful if the opening mechanisms in the vehicle have failed.

High-Angle Rope Rescue

Sometimes river rescue also requires vertical rescue. Being trained in high-angle rope rescue is a great next step towards becoming a more complete river rescue technician. There are many credible training organizations out there offering this valuable skill set, and if you're interested, you should examine this discipline further. Many rope systems will overlap with those covered in this textbook. The biggest difference will be that vertical rescue is often focused on patient rescue and therefore requires much more redundancy in anchors and systems. Mechanical advantage systems covered in this book focus on recovering boats and gear in the horizontal realm and therefore do not have as stringent guidelines for redundancy.

Practice mechanical advantage systems on dry land to keep things simple and clear during the learning process. Reinforce learning with frequent practice. CLAUDIO VEGA

CHAPTER 19

LEADERSHIP ON THE RIVER

Leadership and Decision-Making

This leadership section is designed to help rescuers learn, act as role models, and teach leadership for optimal student education and experience in the river environment. While a NOLS course is the primary resource for learning and teaching the core NOLS leadership curriculum, this section is included to summarize our basic progression. More information on the NOLS leadership philosophy is contained in the *Leadership Educator Notebook*.

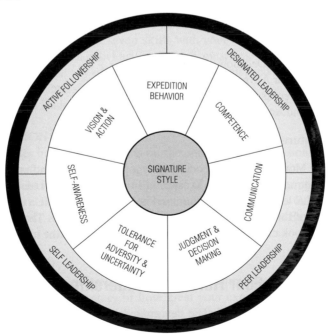

just mean technical skills—it also speaks to leadership and risk management skills as well. Avoid satisfaction in your present skills, and continue to raise the bar on yourself. Demonstrate integrity by walking your own talk and practicing regularly. Ideally, we strive to reach proficiency in our skills and avoid settling for competency.

COMMUNICATION

We can all relate to the concept that it is one thing to possess knowledge and an entirely different thing to be able to communicate that effectively with others. Verbal contributions to meetings, trainings, briefings, and debriefings are a responsibility of all team members. Raise your hand high, speak with conviction, and share what is on your mind. Support effective communication with structured feedback and coaching sessions. Embrace conflict as a healthy aspect of team growth and experiment with tools that will launch your group forward. Express your needs, identify with your actions honestly, and provide others with timely and growth-oriented feedback.

JUDGMENT AND DECISION-MAKING

Be transparent with your decision-making so others can develop their style and provide you with feedback on yours. This book has focused heavily on judgment and decision-making. It is important to remember that we often see good judgment come from bad judgment. We can avoid episodes of bad judgment by training regularly to determine our acceptable level of risk. The more terrain we practice rescuing in, the more confident and informed our decisions can become.

Heuristics

Our brains take short cuts all the time. This is a good thing, but it can also be a bad thing. Neural pathways can be re-routed to speed up our decisions with familiar choices or actions that we commonly make. This makes things like walking or throwing a rope a much easier task if we've done it a few thousand times before. Becoming faster and more proficient with our decisions can lead into some traps, though. Automatic responses neglect recent input or analysis of present factors, and so these neural shortcuts can be costly. NOLS instructor Ian McCammon identifies six common decision-making traps or heuristic traps using the acronym SFACES:

Social proof. *"Everyone else is doing it."* If everyone else is doing it, then you might assume the risk to be lower yourself. If others have swam across this rapid before, your group might think they can do it too without analyzing all the information available in front of them.

Familiarity. *"I've been here before."* If an element of your situation is familiar, then you might perceive it as less risky. You believe you have more control of your circumstances than you actually do.

Acceptance. *"I want to be liked."* The more you want your group or specific individuals to like and respect you, the more you should question your potential for making sound decisions. Being accepted in the group is important, but not at the expense of sound judgment and adequate analysis of your skills and acceptable level of risk.

Commitment. *"There is no turning back after making this decision, and I'm not open to new discussion."* This trap can make rescuers unavailable to process new information that becomes available after the decision is made. Sticking with your decision is only an impressive trait in certain situations.

Expert halo. *"Experts have done it and didn't say not to."* Just because the expert executed their attempt, and you want to be like the expert, doesn't mean that you can or should do what they just did. The other aspect of this trap is confusing being an expert in one discipline as an indication of future success in another discipline.

Scarcity. *"It's now or never."* When there is a closing window of opportunity, be mindful of decisions that emphasize the time is now. When this is present, rescuers can be more willing to endure higher risks while also overseeing significant hazards.

SELF-AWARENESS

Be able to assess and account for your skills and abilities. Test yourself on a regular basis using the Proficiency Accountability Log in the next chapter. Facilitate formal and informal feedback sessions with team members in both group and individual settings. Seek out information about yourself in the form of conversations, feedback forms, and videos and photographs of your skills. Reflect on all this, and capture it in a journal to provide valuable insight as to any progress you achieve. Understand and acknowledge your abilities and limitations on the river. Have the courage to state values and limits.

TOLERANCE FOR ADVERSITY AND UNCERTAINTY

In an age where we expect everything to work on schedule and for problems to be solved promptly, the adversity and uncertainty of a river environment have a lot to teach us. Challenge is adventure. Embrace difficult times in a rescue when things don't go as planned. Don't become a stress pot of chaos and emotion. The scene already inherently has too much of that going on. Stay cool, spread calm, and enjoy the process of discovering what does and does not work. Very seldom will you finish a river rescue and feel as though you did everything perfectly. What a great thing. There should always be a carrot for us to chase into the future to aid us in avoiding complacency. Have a specific question during the debrief be, "What was the most challenging aspect of this mission for you? How did you manage that, and what would you do differently next time?" Remind one another that you're human, you're capable of mistakes, and you're deserving of forgiveness. If you are of the opinion that your performance was mistake-free, then it's time to reconsider the leadership skill set of self-awareness and ask yourself about your own level of honesty.

VISION AND ACTION

Leaders assure the group vision is understood and rests on strong shared values. They have the ability to weigh goals versus consequences as they enact their plans and stay open and flexible to change. Leaders initiate while responding to change and new information adroitly. Helping rescuers understand this in the river environment—especially the impact of clarity, or lack of it in expectations and goals—is invaluable in preparing them for future missions.

One Signature Style

The last component of the 4-7-1 Leadership Model is the concept of "one signature style." How do you execute the seven leadership skills within each of the four leadership roles? Your personality and natural strengths inform your signature style. High-performing rescuers have a default leadership style that works best for them but are still capable of adapting to the needs of the group and mission at hand. Depending on the situation, and their particular role, they move around from one leadership role to the next while still maintaining balance of the seven leadership skills. Improving this capacity requires intentional learning and processing. Remain hungry for more tricks of the trade, and solicit as much insight from as many different leaders as possible. Develop a storehouse of strategies to employ as the situation dictates, and create a toolbox with a variety of options.

CHAPTER 20

PROFICIENCY ACCOUNTABILITY LOGS

Accountability Avoids Complacency

Recording individual and team progress is a simple yet powerful method for altering your team's culture of risk management. Consider using the following template to aid you in capturing the progress of your growth. Shared online documents and team websites make it easy for team members to track one another's progress. Schedule multiple training sessions per year, and use auto-reminder emails to ensure this goal is met.

Our tools in the shed require regular sharpening. Avoid the rust. Train often. Make it fun.

DISCUSSIONS AND ACTIVITIES AFFECTING TEAM CULTURE OF RISK MANAGEMENT & RIVER RESCUE PRINCIPLES

Date	Notes on discussion or activity

Rescue Skills Accountability Log

Under the column labeled, "Date/Location/Execution," log the date, location, and the appropriate letter to indicate how that skill was addressed.

P = Practiced
D = Discussed
O = Observed (another's demo or video)
R = Read/Researched

Skill	Date/Location/Execution: Ex: 6/12/18 Smith Creek "P," 7/15/19 River Base "D"

Shallow Water Crossings

Individual techniques

Paired techniques

Group techniques

Swimming Competencies

Defensive swims

Aggressive swims

Swiftwater entries

Strong swimmer & live bait

Spinal precautions in water

Unresponsive patients

Skill	Date/Location/Execution: Ex: 6/12/18 Smith Creek "P," 7/15/19 River Base "D"

Anchor Systems

Shore-based load-sharing

Boat-based load-distributing

Boat-based anchor points

Mechanical Advantage Systems & Extrication

Strong-arm techniques

3-5-9 simple & compound

4:1 compound pig-rig

Tensioned diagonal/zip line

Telfer lower

Managing Entrapment: Rescue & Recoveries

Entrapment guidelines

Heads-up stabilization

Heads-down extrication

CHAPTER 21

TRANSFER OF SKILLS

Lifelong Learning of Rescue Skills

After reading this book, you may be asking yourself: *Where do I go from here? How well would I respond in an emergency on the river?* It's important to understand that successful rescues are a result of infinite variables, but the following factors play a part in many victories.

Training to avoid complacency. Be sure to take a two- or three-day swiftwater rescue course. Identify the risks within the environment you intend to travel in. Understand what specific skill sets you need to manage risk well and actively seek out training. Remember to preplan your trips by training for the worst and hoping for the best.

Practice and continuing education. Practice these skill sets on a regular basis to maintain proficiency and to avoid complacency. Stay current

National Park Service rangers practicing tethered rescue swims.

An injured patient mid-river presents a complex situation. MOE WHITSCHARD

on new rescue equipment and techniques by getting involved with paddling clubs, books, and resources on the Internet. Remember to revisit the basic skills often so that you will have a higher probability of success when attempting advanced systems.

Judgment and decision-making. This simply comes with time and experience. Travel with experienced, talented people to keep your learning curve steep and on track. Debrief all rescue situations to learn from others in your group and to process the complexity of an emergency response. Read up on whitewater incident reports.

Equipment acquisition. Good rescues are performed with the right equipment. You get what you pay for. Know what is reasonable and prudent to carry with you, and be sure to have it and practice with it regularly.

Good fortune. Mature rescuers realize that even with all the best equipment and training in the world, tragedies still happen. And that doesn't necessarily mean that it is their fault. Perhaps the best rescue is the

A pinned kayak in the middle of technical Class V rapid. Would you know what to do?

In building mechanical advantage systems, practicing details matters.

one that is never needed. Focus on prevention as much as possible, and realize this is one of your most important leadership traits.

Stay cool, spread calm, and embrace your fear. Rescue emergencies can be frightening and emotionally charged. One of the greatest elements a rescuer can bring to the scenario is a cool, calm, and collected demeanor. It can be virtually impossible in some scenarios to eliminate emotional

Risk management is a culture, not a checklist.

involvement altogether, but it is still imperative to spread as much calm as possible in the immediate environment. This doesn't mean don't be scared. Fear is good. Embrace you fear, and channel your energy in a positive direction.

Tolerate the uncertainties. Perhaps in addition to reading this book, you've also taken a complete swiftwater rescue course but are still feeling a twinge of inadequacy when it comes to certain skill sets. Cherish those feelings, embrace your inadequacies, and use them as fuel to push you closer to proficiency. Realize we never fully arrive at perfection in rescue, but spend our lives in relentless pursuit of it. Enjoy this process and treasure the questions themselves. The real key to success is never being satisfied with your present state of knowledge or ability. Stay hungry for more learning, open to new ideas, and have fun playing in, on, and around rivers.

The Bottom Line

We train so we can provide quality care for people in need. Sticking to basics and your practiced systems, keeping skills up-to-date with refresher training, using situational awareness, and keeping your cool will help you respond with confidence and skill in an emergency. We'll see you on the river!

Index

Page numbers in italics indicate photographs and illustrations.

258 NOLS River Rescue Guide